DOWN THE
Wildlife, History,

G000160961

CHRISTOPHER MORIARTY is a naturalist and fisheries expert. He is author of *On Foot in Dublin and Wicklow: Exploring the Wilderness*, *Ireland: Byways Rather than Highways: Exploring Ireland's Hidden Places* and *Exploring Dublin: Wildlife, Parks, Waterways*. He is co-author with Elizabeth Healy and Gerard O'Flaherty of *The Book of the Liffey: from source to the sea*. His love for places where people are free to wander has led him to collect a treasure-trove of information on what there is to see, and why it is there. His work as a fishery scientist, together with his qualifications in geology and botany, gives him a special expertise on river flora and fauna. He writes skilfully and with enthusiasm about his favourite subject.

To Cherry and Marion

By the same author
(all published by Wolfhound Press)

On Foot in Dublin and Wicklow: Exploring the Wilderness
Exploring Dublin: Wildlife, Parks, Waterways
Ireland: Byways Rather than Highways

The Book of the Liffey: from source to the sea
(co-author with E. Healy ed., G. O'Flaherty, et. al.)

Down the Dodder

Wildlife, History, Legend, Walks

Christopher Moriarty

Photographs by the author
Illustrations and maps by Ruairi Moriarty

WOLFHOUND PRESS
& in the US and Canada
The Irish American Book Company

Reprinted with update 1998

First published 1991
Wolfhound Press Ltd
68 Mountjoy Square
Dublin 1, Ireland
Tel: (353-1) 874 0354
Fax: (353-1) 872 0207

Published in the US and Canada by
The Irish American Book Company
6309 Monarch Park Place
Niwot, Colorado 80503
USA
Tel: (303) 652-2710
Fax: (303) 652-2689

British Library Cataloguing in Publication Data
A catalogue record for this book is available from the British Library.

ISBN 0-86327-286-X

Cover design: Jan de Fouw
Maps and line drawings: Ruairi Moriarty
Photographs by the author
Typesetting and layout: Redsetter Ltd., Dublin
Printed in the Republic of Ireland by Colour Books, Dublin.

CONTENTS

Acknowledgements

The list of people who have provided information or books and papers or both is a long one. I pay a special tribute to the officials of Dublin Corporation and County Council who have been so very willing to share their profound knowledge of the river and its valley and whose dedicated work has achieved such excellent results. My heartfelt thanks to:

Nick Beale, Christy Boylan, Mary Clarke, Gabriel Cleary, Frank Coffey, Willie Corby, Eamonn Cusack, Aubrey Flegg, Pat Fulham, John Gageby, Anna Germain, Patricia Goodwillie, Maurice Harmon, Douglas Hyde, Michael Keating, Fergus Kelly, Jack Keys, Michael Lynch, Sean MacGowan, Redmond O'Hanlon, John O'Neill, Frank O'Reilly, Peter O'Reilly, Aengus O'Rourke, June R. Roberts, Jim Shannon, Michael Viney, Willie Warren, Thomas R Webster, Jane Williams and to the Dublin City Archivist and the library staff of the Geological Survey of Ireland, the Royal Irish Academy and the Folklore Department, University College, Dublin.

Ruth Lunnon, who studied the distribution of otters in County Dublin in 1989 and 1990, kindly allowed me to quote from her results. Evelyn Moorkens, who used to teach in a school in the Dodder valley and who inspired her pupils to make a study of the Firhouse region, very generously shared all her source material with me. Sylvia Reynolds accompanied me on a number of walks by the river to teach me how to identify the wild flowers. Peter O'Reilly, Dublin Corporation Waterworks Department, guided me on a very helpful tour of the Bohernabreena Waterworks and read and commented on Chapter 2. Christy Boylan and Michael Lynch respectively of the Corporation and County Council Parks Departments also read and commented on the chapters within their jurisdictions. All of them provided invaluable information. Christy Boylan kindly provided me with his article on Herbert Park published in a leaflet by Dublin Corporation Parks Department. Permission for Austin Clarke's 'On a bright morning' given by R Dardis Clarke, 21 Pleasants St, Dublin 8. The publishers are grateful for the co-operation of Smurfit Paper Mills.

Preface

This book describes a journey down the Dodder, from its source on Kippure, highest of the Dublin Mountains, to its union with Anna Liffey at Ringsend. The journey is a slow one because there is so much to stop and see, because the scenery needs explanations and because the valley is packed with history. The river in places runs wild and free, in others it has been taken in hand by man: sometimes in self defence to curb its exuberance, sometimes in schemes to add to the creature comforts of the citizens.

The river meanders and so does my story: past and present are inextricably enmeshed. The granite rock of the Dodder valley seethed in a cauldron beneath the crust of the earth five hundred million years ago. A tropical ocean covered the land and the land emerged again. Glaciers came and went. Finn MacCool hunted there, Oisín came back to it in the time of St Patrick. Victorian engineers replaced a lake which had vanished ten thousand years before their day. Sand martins fly above the water and otters hunt beneath. The wonders of the valley cannot be separated from each other and I make only a half-hearted apology for jumping from remote geological time to functional engineering works, from the reality of the kingfisher to the mystery of Celtic legend. The sole link in my story is the inexorable journey of the river.

Introduction

Origins

The Dodder is one of the two rivers which rise in County Wicklow on the slopes of Kippure; the other is the Liffey. Their headwaters are a few paces apart and there the resemblance ends. From its highest point the Liffey flows southwards and then goes nearly in a circle to end in Dublin Bay after a journey of 138 km or 86 miles. The Dodder heads north, promptly leaves Wicklow for Dublin and enters the Bay beside the Liffey at Ringsend, having travelled no more than 29 km or 18 miles.

Name and nature

Books on the place names of Ireland are coy as to the derivation of 'Dodder'. It was called *Dothra* in Old Irish and there is a theory that this was an adjective meaning 'turbulent' or 'violent'. A more dramatic possibility is that the name, like those of other Irish rivers, was already established before the Celts came and therefore cannot be interpreted by Gaelic scholars. The geographical nature of the river is also an unresolved question. Is it a tributary of the Liffey or a river in its own right? The Dodder flowed directly to the sands of Dublin Bay until the 18th century and therefore paid no tribute to its larger sibling. Then engineering works lengthened the Liffey and confined the Dodder between stone walls within its estuary.

For all its small size, the Dodder is a stream of great character. The enchanted valley of Glenasmole caught the attention of the earliest Irish storytellers. Monasteries were built beside the river and waterworks were well established when the first historical reference to one of the weirs was set down in 1244. Several writers in the 17th century referred with awe to the Dodder's propensity for spectacular flooding — floods which have remained beyond human control to the present day.

Harnessing the waters

But the bounty of the Dodder has been more significant than its turbulence. In the days of Celtic legend the valley formed a highway through the forest. Subsequently, water mills were established to the number of 28 in the year 1844: 14 on the main river, 14 on the City Watercourse which led from Firhouse to St James's Gate. A list of 45 'mills' existing in 1879 includes a number of factories which were not actually powered by water.

The greatest undertaking on the river took place between 1883 and 1887 when the reservoirs in Glenasmole were created: primarily to conserve water to power the 28 mills, the supply of domestic water for Rathmines and Rathgar being a secondary consideration. The construction of the waterworks took place at a happy time when stone-masons and wrought-iron masters still flourished so that the entirely functional design became a thing of beauty in its own right.

Farther downstream bridges were built, sturdy and graceful creations in cut stone. The mills one by one fell out of use so that little remains but half-forgotten sluice gates and abandoned mill streams. But the weirs which controlled the water levels remain, forming sparkling waterfalls and maintaining deep and silent pools where trout rise and kingfishers and herons hunt their prey.

The headwaters of the Dodder flow through a lonely wilderness, then comes the artificial but peaceful area of the lakes of Glenasmole. For a few miles the river runs through pasture where old farmsteads survive. But this region is gradually being diminished as the suburbs of Dublin creep ever outwards. Finally the river becomes a part of the inner city.

A life-line

Although the Dodder has thus been dammed and otherwise constrained over more than half its length, it, by the grace of God, was spared the fate of other Dublin rivers which were totally enclosed in masonry and hidden from sight beneath the roads. The Dodder remains an open river, with banks where wild flowers grow and where in

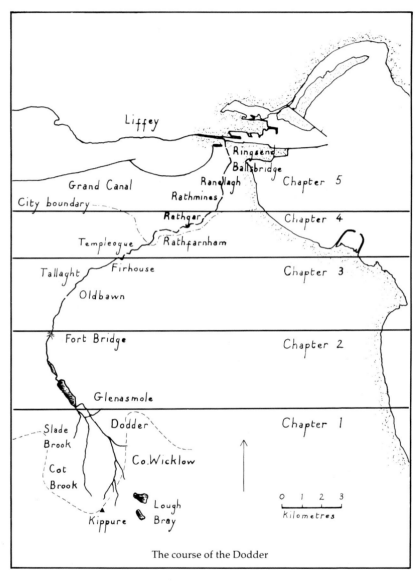

The course of the Dodder

places, even within the city, unkempt trees and shrubs have made a veritable jungle. So it acts as a life-line, bringing wild plants and birds and other creatures to brighten the most heavily built-up areas.

Thousands of citizens have appreciated its beauty over

many generations. Official notice of the priceless asset which the valley forms dates from the Abercrombie Plan of 1941. The plan envisaged the reservation of 'parkway strips' along the Dodder from Ballsbridge to Old Bawn. This has been achieved over the greater part of the riverside and even extended downstream of Ballsbridge nearly all the way to the Liffey at Ringsend. In spite of setbacks, the scheme continues to advance and it is possible to walk by the riverside for many miles.

The chapters which follow describe the river and its surroundings from source to sea. To give even an outline account of the history and natural history of the entire Dodder valley would require several volumes and therefore this book confines itself strictly to what can be seen from the banks of the main river. This is why subjects such as the history and buildings of Tallaght, Rathfarnham and many other entities receive no more than comment in passing. I have also purposely refrained from dwelling on the negative aspects of certain dismal parts of the river: on the corpses of cars, the abandoned trolleys and the rubbish which festoons the branches of the willow trees. Unlike the flowers and birds and rocks and ruins, the rubbish can be removed and will be as soon as those who live in the valley unite to demand the necessary action.

Discovering the Dodder

The following chapters describe the course of the river from its source without explaining how to approach the upper reaches. This section gives directions to some of the more or less hidden parts.

The headwaters require a mildly energetic mountain walk. The easiest approach is by taking the path from the Military Road to the Kippure television mast (see map, page 16). A little less than 2 km from the RTE gate there is a bridge where the path crosses a stream. This stream is the highest tributary of the Liffey and you follow it till it gets lost in the bog. About 300 paces from this point in a slightly west of south direction, you find Tromanallison on the 645 metre contour: the first of two branches of the infant Dodder. The second is found by climbing to the summit of Kippure and following the dry gully described at the beginning of the next chapter.

The dam which diverts the Dodder towards the Cot Brook is rather well hidden. The canal which carries the diverted stream runs beneath the road exactly half a mile (800m) south of Cunard (see map, page 17). A footpath by the canal leads southeastwards to the dam. Upstream of that the Dodder flows over waterfalls large and small through its finest gorge. Go there in spring when gorse and broom are in flower and before the bracken makes walking difficult. The canal flows for about 400 paces under two stone bridges to meet the Cot Brook which flows to the upper lake. Again a footpath follows most of the route. All of this land is private property, though the owners by and large tolerate occasional visitors.

There are three entrances to the reservoirs: one at Fort Bridge, the others on either side of the river at the lower Castlekelly Bridge immediately to the south of the upper lake. A permit is required to enter the Corporation property which surrounds the lakes. Permits are willingly granted by the Dublin Corporation Waterworks Department, Marrowbone Lane, Dublin 2.

Between Fort Bridge and Old Bawn most of the riverside is cattle pasture and privately owned. Access on the right bank is rendered extremely difficult by chain-link fence and barbed wire. Only a purist, determined to walk all the way down the river, has any real need to follow this reach. Generally speaking the parts of the lower valley which are public property are both more interesting and more pleasant to walk along.

All the way downstream from Old Bawn, bridges cross the Dodder at very frequent intervals and the bank on one side or the other can be approached easily from them. There is an unobtrusive gateway to the right bank in the upper car park at Rathfarnham Shopping Centre and another fairly well-concealed entrance in Herbert Park — otherwise the approaches to the Dodder need no special mention. To a greater degree than any other river in Ireland, large or small, the Dodder is the property of the people: the most densely populated, the least exclusive and the most welcoming.

CHAPTER 1

Castlekelly — the mountain stream

The Dodder rises on the 630 metre contour and plunges down to Castlekelly Bridge, descending by 451 metres in the course of a 5 km journey. The upper valley is a wilderness of moorland with rocky gorges and waterfalls, a haunt of deer and grouse and ravens. About 4 km from the source the land changes dramatically to rolling green pastures with farmsteads, sheep and cattle and even peacocks. In the lower valley a small weir marks the beginnings of the taming of the wild Dodder.

Sources

The Dodder begins its pilgrimage just below the summit of Kippure. At the summit the peat, which once covered the mountain like a blanket, has been worn away in patches to reveal a shining gravel of quartz and mica crystals. In other parts the peat remains, but stripped bare, the heather which once covered it confined to small ridges here and there. It is an inhospitable spot, a habitation of television engineers, occasionally visited by ravens and by sheep which find little cushions of grass growing in places on the gravel.

To the east of the summit lies the highest tributary of the Liffey and north northeast a deep gully in the peat heads straight down the hill in the direction of the Dodder. In rainy weather it is occupied by a stream, but within days the flow ceases and the bed is dry enough to walk on in comfort. About 2 metres deep at its upper end, the flanks of the gully are bare peat. Heather moor covers the ground above it while on the floor there is gravel with patches of moss and grass. The moss is the beautiful *Polytrichum* whose dark green fronds look like miniature pine trees.

The scholar Patrick Weston Joyce postulated the presence of a yew tree on those barren slopes:

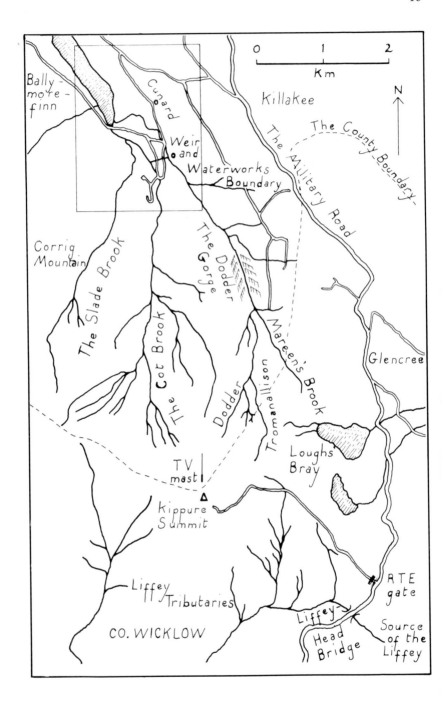

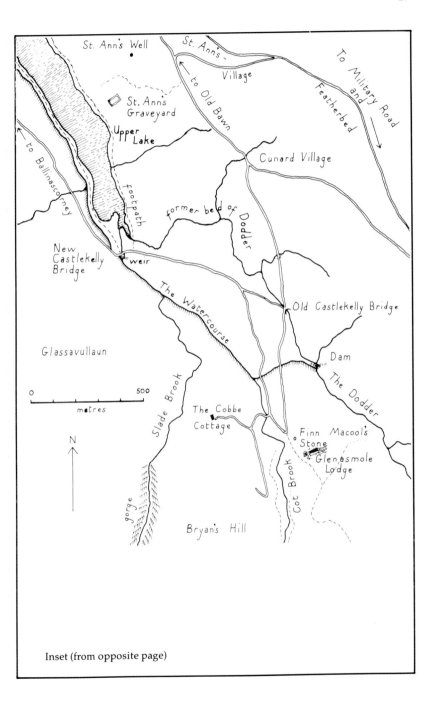

Inset (from opposite page)

What gave name to Kippure mountain, from the slopes of which the rivers Liffey and Dodder run down to the Dublin plain, it is now hard to say with certainty; but probably it was so called from the remains of some large old yew, for the name exactly represents *Cip-iubhair*, the trunk of the yew.

However, the chances of a large yew — or even a small one — growing on the slopes of Kippure are remote and this may have encouraged Liam Price to seek a more reasonable derivation. He suggested *Ciop mhór*, 'a great place of mountainy grass' and that sounds a lot better.

Mountain flowers

As you go down the hill the deep gully widens in places and blocks of granite appear on the floor. The pale blue-green branching lichen *Cladonia* grows on some of the stones, sometimes displaying its tiny blobs of crimson fruit, incongruous dots of vivid colour in surroundings of greys and browns. And, even though Kippure is no more than 753 metres high, there are Alpine plants up here: cowberry and starry saxifrage.

Cowberry

Cowberry is a drab name for a little plant whose scientific name *Vaccinium vitis-idaea* translates more romantically as 'vine of Mount Ida'. It grows very near the summit of Kippure and in winter the yellow-green leaves stand out against the brown of the heather. In summer the pink, bell-shaped flowers bloom and later it produces big red, but sour, berries. In County Dublin the sight of cowberry growing wild is reserved strictly for hill-walkers: it never decends below the 2,000 foot contour.

The starry saxifrage is an even more exclusive species. While cowberry occurs on several of the hills above Glenasmole, this tiny plant with white, star-like flowers in County Dublin grows nowhere but in the valley of the Dodder. Look for it in patches of sphagnum or spreading

over the rocks in the stream bed anywhere between the
ravine at the summit of Kippure and the fence of
Glenasmole Lodge.

The infant Dodder

The first trickle in the bed of the gully looks as if it might
be the infant Dodder. But it doesn't quite qualify because
it suddenly plunges underground into a small cavern with
a floor of gravel, about 2 metres below the surface. It is easy
to follow the direction of the cavern and in a little while a
new stream appears, making another valley: first a shallow
ditch with a bed of peat, getting deeper as it goes until it
reaches the gravel. The running water disappears from
view once more but this time it stays above ground, losing
itself in a swamp of sphagnum and rushes.

A stream ultimately breaks out again, issuing from a
tunnel in the peat, and flowing over large granite boulders.
The highest rushes of the mountainside appear and the
little valley broadens into a swamp about 5 metres across,
green with sheets of sphagnum moss. Then the stream
descends quite steeply, in a series of steps: green swamps
alternating with tiny waterfalls.

Now comes a very definite winding valley with little
spurs of peat on either side: about the most definite
looking river so far. On the moor there is much less
heather, the dominant plant being deer grass, a sedge
which grows in little tufts and turns a beautiful golden
colour in winter. It indicates damper conditions than the
purely heather-clad slopes. Cross-leaved heath is also
plentiful.

The river here has really found its identity and makes a
noise like a proper stream, as it flows through big patches
of rush. Then begins a much steeper descent over a stony
bed. Bell heather grows on the side slopes and the stream
flows over and around increasingly large boulders.

The valley grows deeper, down to 10 metres and more
and the sides become steep, forming the first of a series of
gorges. A branch from the right joins the stream just above
the highest outcrop of solid rock. The right hand branch is
called Tromanallison and it has an almost equal claim to be
the true source of the Dodder, rising a little way to the

northeast of the summit of Kippure. Tromanallison also has the distinction of flowing for 800 metres through County Wicklow, thwarting thereby the Dodder's attempts to be an unadulterated Dubliner. Below the meeting of these waters, the stream plunges over the first real waterfall which is also the site of the first tree on the Dodder, a lonely rowan sapling scarcely meriting the designation of tree.

Granite and peat

The solid rock below the peat and gravel is granite, the material which forms the core of the great mountain chain extending from Dublin to the Blackstairs in Wexford. Kippure, the highest of the Dublin Mountains, stands at the edge of it. The granite was formed some four hundred million years ago during the Caledonian phase of mountain building which crumpled this part of the earth's crust along a northeast-southwest axis. The rock passed through a molten state and crystallized as it cooled. Because it was very deeply buried at the time, the cooling process was slow and the crystals had time to grow big enough to be easy to see. Crystals of three minerals make up the greater part of granite: quartz, white and translucent, mica, black or white but always in thin, shiny flakes and feldspar, white, rather dull and easily weathered.

In the course of time the overlying rocks were worn away so that, when the ice age began, the granite was exposed to the action of a succession of mountain glaciers. The last of these, finally melting away some ten thousand years ago, left the upper slopes covered with a rubble of large and small lumps of granite. The glaciers also had something of a sandpapering effect on the landscape, giving the mountains gentle slopes and rounded tops and straightening out the valleys such as Glenasmole.

The chemical composition of the granite, rich in silica, devoid of lime, gives rise to acidic conditions as it weathers. Few plant species can thrive in an acid soil: both growth and decay take place very slowly. Four or five thousand years ago the rainfall was greater than nowadays and, in the waterlogged soil, decay of the plants after they died was so gradual that they were not completely removed. Instead, they formed peat which first filled the spaces between the stones and then accumulated to form, in the case of Kippure, a blanket often 2 metres deep, sometimes more where it grew in small hollows.

Moorland

The peat blanket is far from uniform. Indeed, on the summit of Kippure it is no longer stable and the rain is very slowly wearing it away, leaving the surface scored with the deep gullies. On the slopes some areas are relatively dry and on these heather is the dominant plant, mostly the small-flowered ling but in places the more spectacular purple bell heather. In other parts the ground is damper and there the heather family is represented by cross-leaved heath, a more straggly species with pink bell flowers. With the heath, bog cotton grows, a sedge named from the tufts of white cottony fruits that appear in late summer. In winter its leaves turn to a beautiful red colour. Rushes are also plentiful. Perhaps the most beautiful plant of the damp moorland is the bog asphodel whose vivid yellow, star-like flowers bloom in July and August.

Bell heather

Birds are few on the highlands. Winter and summer the wren is the commonest species. Meadow pipit and skylark nest there; raven and hooded crow fly over from time to time and some grouse survive, even though the systematic burning of the heather to make way for grass for the sheep has reduced their habitat. But there is one wonderful bird which embodies the spirit of the mountain stream. The dipper, quite small and dressed in black plumage with a snowy white bib, rejoices in the splashing water. It perches on stones, often singing a gentle song, resting between foraging expeditions. The dipper feeds mainly on the insects which creep about on the submerged stones. Sometimes it snatches them from above, but it has the rare accomplishment of being able to go down into the water and walk about on the bottom.

Deer grass continues to be the dominant

plant on the moorland, but on the valley slopes where the rainwater can run off quickly, bell heather grows and bracken makes its first appearance amongst patches of grass. On the left bank a little farther downstream there is a high cliff of granitic gravel, stained brown with iron, standing on top of a rock outcrop. Then comes the confluence with Mareen's Brook. Rowan trees appear again, this time much bigger and stronger than the little sapling higher up.

The stones in the river bed are mostly granite, with occasional lumps of quartz. But there is a curious intruder in the form of a porphyry: a fine-grained igneous rock scattered with coarse crystals, in this case whitish crystals on a bluish base. The nearest outcrop is on Ballymorefinn, 4 kilometres to the northwest. Therefore it cannot have been carried by the mountain glacier which flowed northwards from the summit of Kippure. It was brought here, according to Francis Synge, by the much older Munsterian ice field which covered the whole of Ireland except for the highest mountains.

The Dodder gorge

With the contribution of the two higher branches and Mareen's Brook, the river is now undoubted Dodder. It runs steeply down through an increasingly deep and narrow

Dipper

gorge, plunging over little waterfalls and rushing around very large boulders and substantial rock outcrops. Rowans become more plentiful and birch then appears, together with hazel and holly and even a trace of honeysuckle. Some of the birches are very old ones with massive trunks, some are dead and fallen, some dying, others very much alive. The steep slopes are covered largely by grass and bracken; with heather moor above. Hard fern and polystichum grow in places by the banks and there are little tufts of heather.

The cutting of such a steep-sided and narrow valley would have been far beyond the powers of the Dodder. It owes its existence to the fury of torrential floods of melt water, first from the ice cap and later from the snow fields which covered the mountain towards the end of the ice age. At the lower end of the gorge, the finest natural waterfall of the upper Dodder is hidden away. The stream plunges in a series of four falls and pools, 6 metres or so in height. Scarcely a Niagara, it has a charm of its own and a feeling of remoteness, even though the road to the hamlet of Castlekelly passes less than a mile away.

Downstream of the waterfall, at a place called Mary's Cliff, the land on the ground on the right bank becomes more rocky and two steep side streams run down, almost in straight lines. On the left bank a magnificent oak tree grows and below it rhododendrons begin, becoming more plentiful as you go down. From the edge of the gorge you can see the land opening out and the vegetation changes abruptly, from moorland to pasture, the boundary marked by a line of tall trees: Scots pine, larch and silver fir.

There is a wire fence here too, and that is very significant. There was very little point in building fences on the moorland. The grazing rights were often held in common, though in the case of the Dodder and Liffey valleys much of the land was actually part of the Powerscourt estate. The pastures and arable soil of the lower land, on the other hand, have been exclusive farm property and the owners assiduously kept their stock within fences.

This is a good place to pause and reflect on the history of the landscape.

fern

The trail of the glaciers

Happenings in the course of the last cold period of the great Ice Age go a long way towards explaining the appearance of the Dodder valley. The first great ice field, the Munsterian, had filled the valley and extended high up the slopes, to about 360 metres. That ice melted away and was followed by an 'interglacial' warm period with a climate similar to what we more or less enjoy at present.

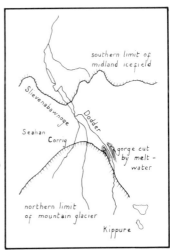

Then came the next major advance of the ice which ended ten thousand years ago. This, the Midlandian, did not invade the whole valley but stopped a little way north of the hamlet of St Ann's. It impounded a great lake which is described in the next chapter. At about the same time as the Midlandian ice field was flowing southwards, Kippure was the centre of a mountain glacier whose ice flowed down over the upper reaches of Glenasmole.

Glaciers scrape up rocks from the surface they pass over, grind some of them to powder and carry others along: the farther they are carried the more they get ground down. When the ice melts, the rock material is dumped all over the land surface. This is the 'glacial till'. The most characteristic feature of till is that large boulders, stones of all sizes, gravel and clay co-exist. There are masses of sand and clay in which the stones and rocks are embedded. Water-borne material by contrast is well sorted: boulders are scarcely moved, stones are carried where the water is swift and then dumped. Gravel particles are carried farther than the stones and silt farther still.

The important point in the development of the Dodder valley is that the southward-flowing glaciers filled the upper valley with till and also coated the lowlands with a thick blanket of it. Ever since the ice melted away, the Dodder has been engaged in cutting its way down through the till to find its old valley once more.

Landscaping

On the right bank close to the fence, nearly opposite the big silver fir, the river has cut into the bank to expose a small section of glacial till. It is mostly granite but contains porphyry and slate and was deposited by the last of the mountain glaciers. This is nearly the highest point for foxgloves: they like well-drained banks and the glacial gravel provides this. The good drainage also allows grass rather than heather and sedges to grow and so the moorland ends and pasture extends from here as far north as the eye can see: across the Liffey valley and away to the Mountains of Mourne.

The rhododendrons are descendants of bushes planted in the 19th century by the owners of Glenasmole Lodge

whose landscaping extended as far as the line of conifers. Rhododendron needs an acid soil and it thrives on the granite-based gravel, where the sheep are fenced out.

The Dodder tumbles on downhill, swirling around white boulders of granite in the river bed. Its propensity for flooding keeps the boulders clean. Their lower parts, submerged most of the time, get coated with algae and any that are big enough to stand permanently above the floods are grey, covered by lichens on top. But there is an in-between zone, too dry for algae and too wet for lichens and these parts of the boulder are well-scrubbed and ever so slowly being eroded by the water. The feldspar matrix dissolves, releasing the crystals of quartz and mica which are carried away downstream. Where the current slackens, they are deposited on the bed as a yellow, shining gravel.

About 100 paces downstream of the fence on the right bank, the boundary between the townlands of Castlekelly on the uplands and Cunard lower down

Foxglove meets the river. Castlekelly has the typically enormous area of a mountain townland: 1,134 hectares. Cunard (*Cuan ard*, a high bend or curve) has the more modest dimensions of townlands on richer agricultural soil, 102 hectares. The Kelly name is buried in the mists of Celtic times, the region being a part of ancient Ó Ceallaigh territory.

Cliff of glacial till

O'Curry and his letters

Long before TV masts grew upon Kippure, before the majority of the people of Castlekelly could read and write and before geologists had even the remotest idea of the antiquity of the mountains, Eugene O'Curry explored the hillside, notebook and sketching pad in hand. In his employment as Antiquarian to the Ordnance Survey, he made three visits to Castlekelly in the summer of 1837 and submitted his reports in the form of letters.

The first reference is an introductory one in the letter of 26 July 1837 and refers to Glenasmole (*the thrush's glen*) rather than to Castlekelly. While the townland of Castlekelly has a boundary clearly marked on the six-inch map, it is difficult to say just where Glenasmole begins and ends. The maps all show it to be the deep gorge now filled by the two lakes of Bohernabreena Waterworks. But O'Curry clearly considered that the glen extends upstream of this, at least as far as the grounds of the Lodge.

> I descended the east side of the mountain into Glen a Smoil — the far famed residence of the mighty Finn Mac Cool. There are many old recollections of him still in this Glen. However, I had not time enough left to make more than a passing enquiry, but expect to collect some curious facts when I visit it again, which I hope to be able to do on Friday next.

The second letter is the most detailed and I quote it in full:

> 21 Great Charles St.,
> 2nd August 1837.
>
> Sir,
>
> Since I wrote to you last I visited Glen a Smoil and the neighbouring mountains twice. I could collect no tradition of Finn Mac Cool or his warriors in the Glen, but what is current all over Ireland. The most remarkable features of this celebrated Glen are the four mountain streams that descend into it and form the River Dodder. The first and largest of these streams, which is called Aill Mháire, or Maureen's Brook, rises in Kippure Mountain near Lough Bray and rolls down a rocky precipitate channel to Castle Kelly in the Glen, a little below

which it meets the Dodder or Aidhin Dothar, a somewhat small stream which takes its rise in a Lough called Tromán Dubh (Black Stream) some distance to the north of Mareen's Brook on Kippure Ridge, and running down through Coill Mhór, receives the stream of Lug Mór immediately before it joins Mareen's Brook at the place already mentioned. The united waters then flow onward, and at a short distance receive the stream of Glaise an Mhuilin which descends from Seechaun Mountain, dividing the Mountain of Carrigeen Roe into two parts. The Glens through which these streams descend have a great many local names among them that I had not time to collect — they are so difficult to ascend, so remote from persons to point out the localities, and so far distant from where I get off and meet the Tallagh Car.

I met an interesting old man at the bottom of the Glen from whom I collected the subjoined list of local names. His name is William Rafter — Uilliam O'Rachtabhra — he is now eighty four years old, with all his faculties in full vigour and with more activity and buoyancy of spirit than his son, a man of about fifty years of age. He was born and bred in the old Castle Kelly, on the foundations of which his house is built and part of the old wall of which may be still seen in the gable of the house. He speaks as good Irish as ever I heard spoken, as does his sister Una. He says that forty years ago very few spoke English in this Glen except the Dublin Carmen, very few men of forty years of age even now in the Glen that don't under-

Rowan trees in winter on the higher slopes.

stand, though they don't speak the Irish. He has no account of O'Kelly from whom the Castle is named, nor have I. He knew many persons who read and wrote Irish, the last of whom was Andrew Smith, Aindrias Ó Gobhan, who died three years ago at Glassamucky on the Glenside.

The following local names are to be found in the Glen and about it:

Cnoc a tSidhain — a tumulus. Glais a Mhuicídhe. Brácaidhe Cón Ard. Sliabh na cCloch. Dochtog. Bun na Trí Tromán. Aill Mháirín. Caislean Ui Cheallaigh. Aidhin Dothair. Troman Dubh. Lug na Fiach. Leó Mhór. Carraig na Síodhóg. Coill Mhór. etc.

As I will have to write to you again more particularly on this subject, I will mention no more names at present.

Aill Mháirín is remarkable for producing (perhaps) the largest ivy leaves anywhere to be found. In the old Finian poem (tale) of Glean-a-Smoil, Ossian, complaining of St. Patrick's scanty fare, says that he would find a quarter of a black bird in Glen-a-Smoil larger than his quarter of mutton, a quicken berry larger than his measgán of butter, and an ivy leaf larger than his griddle of bread. I send you two of the celebrated ivy leaves which, though not arrived at maturity of growth, will yet afford you a good specimen of the produce of the famous Glen.

Can the Name Book of Tallaght be spared? I would want it as soon as it could be spared.

I remain, Sir,
Your obedient servant,
Eugene Curry.

The two leaves which O'Curry dispatched are still preserved in the strongroom of the Royal Irish Academy, pressed and bound in with the manuscript letters and pencil drawings. They are more olive- than ivy-green now, after one hundred and fifty-four years. If not the size of a griddle cake, they are indeed exceptional. The larger of the two is 16cm long by 18cm wide. I looked for the descendants of these outlandish creepers in 1990 but found none: not much ivy anyway and all of it of very ordinary dimensions.

O'Curry's third letter is dated 23rd August 1837:

I went on yesterday to Gleann a Smoil with Mr. Williams and

pointed out to him all the remains of antiquity that I have been able to discover there as yet.

There is a moate on the edge of Feather-Bed Bog called Cnocan Mhéidhbh (Cnockan Mheibh) through which the County boundary line runs. This moate has been cut through to the depth of five feet within the last month, but no grave, stone, urn or anything else turned up but the bog of which the mound is composed. The line or trench does not run exactly through the centre, so that perhaps its contents have yet escaped discovery.

Following the boundary line from this to the foot of Kippure Mountain, at the distance of a mile, it passes through another moat immediately on the brink of Mareen's Brook and very near the head of that stream. The trench has not been dug deep here, so that the mound remains still unbroken. A few yards lower down the stream there is another small mound which has not been opened. These moates have no names.

A little below these a rapid stream falls into Mareen's Brook on the right side, called Eas Caorthain Duinn i.e., Cataract of the Brown Roan Tree. This stream is not marked on the plan.

A little below this and on the other side another stream falls into Mareen's Brook, which the people call Tromán Allison, i.e. Allison's Stream. I can make but little of this name, but will enquire more about it. The point of junction of these three streams is called Bun na Trí Tromán.

A little farther down still is Cnocan Caorthain (of the Roan Tree). This is a large oblong mound of considerable height, with a cairn on its lower end and another at its upper end. Lower down the stream still is Aill Mhaire (Mary's Cliff) where the ivy leaves are to be found. A little lower down yet are three moates more, one of them very large. It is probably a natural mound, modified by man for his own purpose. It is called Cnocán Ruadh. There is a fine bold stream descending into the brook here, which does not appear on the plan and for which I was not able to get a name, as yet. A cromleac a little way up on the mountain side and a few circles further on to the north east, fills up my discoveries on the right side of Mareen's Brook.

Farther down the valley from the boundary of Cunard townland, tall beech trees appear on the high bank above the river. They cast a heavy shade in summer and few plants can grow beneath them. This is probably why the dense thicket of rhododendrons comes to an end and only scattered bushes survive. Sycamore grows with the

beeches and the trees together strengthen the bank
and preserve it from erosion. Sometimes the
river wins the battle for possession of the
bank, uproots entire trees and carries
them away.

Glenasmole ivy leaf. (Actual size)

Taming the Dodder

There is a small heap of stones beside the wooden five-barred gate at the northwestern end of the fence which runs above the river on the right bank. Amongst them one square block of granite bearing a boldly-carved large letter 'W' is firmly set in the ground. The 'W' stands for 'Waterworks' and evidently is a boundary marker. There is another one a little farther down the hill, shaded by a hawthorn tree. Then comes the point where the Dodder ends its career as a free stream, unencumbered by human hand.

A stone-built weir crosses the valley of the Dodder and diverts the river to the left, along a canal lined with stones set in concrete. The weir was built high at its sides with a lower sill which could carry flood water and prevent scouring of the banks. To the right of the weir are the openings of two big earthenware pipes. One of them can be traced to a dam on a small tributary stream a little way up the side of the hill. Its function was to divert this water away from the abandoned bed of the Dodder and into the canal.

The reason for the diversion is that the water of the moorland Dodder in rainy weather becomes peat-stained. That was no more acceptable to the

Waterworks boundary stone

engineers of the time than it would have been to the house-holders of Rathmines and Rathgar into whose taps it might flow. Engineers abhor peaty water because its brown colour comes from humic acids which corrode the insides of their pipelines. The waterworks men planned to use the valley of the Dodder for a drinking water reservoir, but before this could be achieved they had to remove the river. So they made the bypass.

The new channel curves to the left and passes beneath two beautifully made little bridges, each of two stone arches. The bank of the channel rises steeply on the right on to a long spur of glacial material which separates the Dodder from its tributary, the Cot Brook. The rich green pasture down in the valley on the left is based on outwash gravel, carried down from the glacial till by the brook. Between the two bridges the course of the channel is straight and concreted, with three waterfalls at its upper end. Downstream of the lower of the two bridges the diverted Dodder joins the Cot Brook and together they flow between banks of concrete towards the upper lake.

The streams meet in a grove of holly. On the left the Cot Brook comes tumbling down the hill slope, bubbling over large boulders, most of them granite, an idyllic mountain stream. There is a little patch of grass beside it, inviting you to picnic and listen to the song of the river.

Ruth Lunnon did a survey of the distribution of otters in County Dublin and found spraints in the Cot Brook here in January 1990. Spraints are the little black heaps of droppings which otters deposit on stones and other places by the water where they hunt. Since they get washed away or dried up within a matter of days, the presence of spraints proves that these beautiful animals are active in the region. Ireland is now one of the otter's principal strongholds in Europe and it is especially pleasing that they still live so close to the city of Dublin.

Many people are attracted to the upper part of the valley, so much so that the narrow road becomes almost impass-able for about three hours on fine Sunday afternoons in summer. In fact the roads are very much more inviting to walk along than to drive. There is a little parking space by the roadside at Castlekelly Bridge less than a mile down the way.

Glenasmole Lodge

The road into the valley from the more upstream of the two bridges on the diversion leads past the splendid wrought iron gate of the beautiful 19th century house marked as Glenasmole Lodge on the map. Still known locally as Cobbe's Lodge, it replaces an older dwelling called Heath-field, a house with a great deal of history.

The original lodge was built towards the end of the 18th century by George Grierson who held the position of King's Printer under the Dublin Parliament. William Handcock in 1876 had much to say of him:

> George Grierson, the owner of Heathfield Lodge before the Union, is stated to have had an income of about £20,000 a year. During the shooting season he entertained numbers of the nobility and gentry of the country here. It is said that he had six complete dinner services, one for each day, and all were cleaned up on Saturday, ready for the next week. This George Grierson was a very convivial old gentleman, sang a good song, was very witty, and a first rate host. At the time of the Union he received £13,000 compensation, all of which he expended . . . . His three daughters, after his

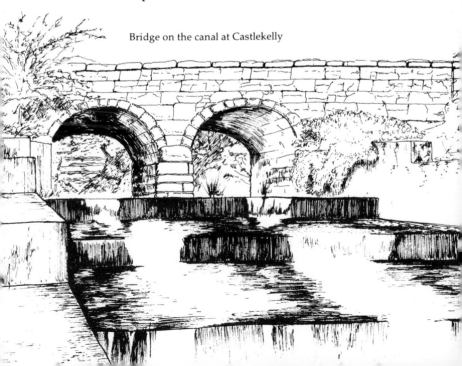

Bridge on the canal at Castlekelly

death lived for many years at Heathfield Lodge, when in
this country. They were great travellers, and visited many
parts of the world . . . They brought back numerous
curiosities to their beautiful mountain home, which
became quite a museum. They altered the house into a
Swiss chalet, with a deep-thatched roof, and balcony round
it of carved woodwork. Inside the ceilings were divided by
beams; the polished floors were covered with the skins of
wild beasts, and antlers of every kind hung round the
walls. The tables were loaded with curiosities. Outside the
doors were mats made of heather in blossom, renewed
daily. The garden contained many rare plants, and magnificent rhododendrons. The last still flourish, and are about
the finest in the county. The three ladies were respected
and beloved by all who knew them. The people of the Glen
looked up to them with the devotion of the old Irish to their
chiefs. In return they spent much of their time in teaching
and visiting among them, and helping forward any of the
young people who showed superior intellect. They introduced wood-carving in the Swiss style; and I have seen
some beautiful specimens of the handiwork of some of
their protégés . . . An accidental fire destroyed the beautiful
cottage. The ladies escaped to a loft over a detached barn,

A calm pool near the headwaters.

whence they watched — with what feelings may be imagined — the destruction of all their treasures. Mr George Grierson [one of their brothers] rebuilt the lodge on a plan drawn by himself. His family is all now dead — more is the pity, as is said. Mr Cobbe is the present owner, and has the place in very good order. He has built cottages for the tenantry all through the valley, and they seem a comfortable class of people.

The same Mr Cobbe also owned extensive lands in north Dublin and a descendant in 1985 sold Newbridge Demesne near Donabate to Dublin County Council to use as a park. Meanwhile, Heathfield, now Cobbe's Lodge, passed through a number of owners who used it entirely as a shooting lodge. The present owners have lived there for thirty years and greatly improved both house and grounds. The overgrowth of rhododendrons has been curtailed and many new trees planted.

A Cobbe cottage

In summer you may be tempted to divert from the river to follow a signpost near Glenasmole Lodge. It points the way up an exceedingly steep and winding track to Glenasmole Restaurant. There you may dine at the weekend in one of the cottages which Cobbe built for his comfortable class of tenantry. The cottage has been enlarged considerably, but the lounge and dining room retain the original massive stone walls and have had their woodwork carefully restored. The slate roof was something of an innovation at the time, taking over from thatch.

The cottage is surrounded by a wonderful collection of exotic animals: several breeds of sheep which provide black and brown wool for weaving, to say nothing of ducks, dogs, geese and ponies — and the view down the valley is wonderful. Dr Aengus O'Rourke, whose father bought the cottage in 1941, has a wealth of information on the local wildlife. Badgers, foxes, rabbits and squirrels all live there, hedgehogs, stoats and various bats have been seen and newts live in the ponds together with the frogs. Pheasants abound and there are even peacocks in the valley down below.

Deer roam the hillside, too: all three of the species which inhabit Ireland. Red deer and sika both come from stock which were reared in a deerpark in Germany in the 19th century whence a Viscount Powerscourt brought them to his estate. They interbreed and few, if any of them, are pure stock. The true 'red' is the magnificent animal which is a native to Ireland and still survives in the mountains around Killarney. They had been brought to extinction in Glenasmole long ago which is why Lord Powerscourt had to import specimens for his deerpark. The red deer was the species hunted by Finn and the Fianna. The sika came originally from Japan and the third species, the fallow deer was brought to Ireland by the Anglo-Normans. All are beautiful and a joy to meet.

Finn, Oisín and Patrick

After passing the front gate of the Lodge the road leads to the back one from which a footpath goes up the mountain by the Cot Brook. Five yards inside the back gate on the left stands Finn MacCool's Stone, a granite boulder which bore a plaque with an inscription set into it by the Griersons. The plaque disappeared a long time ago and all that remains now is the neat rectangular recess. Some books suggest the stone was the cap of a dolmen, but there seems to be no evidence of this. It looks more like a glacial 'erratic', a stone transported for some distance by the ice, one of several similar boulders nearby.

The plaque was broken when Handcock saw it but, fortunately, he met a man who knew the inscription by heart. It is a marvellous example of would-be erudition — or could it have been an expensive April Fool?

Pheasant

Finmakoom, one of the Irish Giants, carried this stone on his shoulder from the opposite mountain on April 1st, 1444 - he was 9 feet 7 inches high, and weighed 44 stone.

The boulder, happily, is marked on the modern six-inch map as Finn MacCool's Stone, thus ensuring it a precise position for posterity. Wherever or however George Grierson came by the date of the alleged carrying of the stone, other parts of the inscription, particularly the gigantic size and strength of Finn, are very interesting and in keeping with the tradition that the people in the Glen in the 19th century — most of them illiterate — were familiar with the Fenian tales. What is more, three of the nearby mountains are named in honour of the hero: Seefin, Seefingan and Ballymorefinn. The Hill of Allen, the Fianna's headquarters, is only 35 km from Glenasmole.

It was in Glenasmole that Finn's son, Oisín, was transformed from immortal hero to an old man, blind and feeble. Oisín, mounted on a white steed, had left his bride Niamh of the Golden Hair in Tír na nÓg, to ride across the waves and visit Ireland. Provided he kept in the saddle and avoided touching the ground he would be free to return to the land of eternal youth. To his disgust he found Ireland inhabited by a race of puny folk to whom the names of Finn and his followers were nothing more than a part of dimly remembered history.

The poem 'The Battle of Gabhra' tells how Oisín scoured the country far and wide in search of his companions, eventually coming to Glenasmole where he saw a group of people trying in vain to lift a great block of granite. With one hand he seized the stone and flung it seven perches from its place. But, while the strain was nothing to Oisín, it was too much for his golden saddle girth which snapped. The white steed bolted, never to be seen again. Oisín fell to the ground and was transformed instantly to a withered old man.

Ultimately he was brought to St Patrick and storytellers for more than a thousand years have delighted in the arguments of the two: the struggle between pagan and Christian, between physical strength and mystical power has inspired writers and poets, culminating in the work of W. B. Yeats. Patrick generally fared badly in the exchanges but had the upper hand of health and strength.

The magic of Glenasmole had survived the deterioration of the people of Ireland. Its wildlife in the time of Patrick evidently was fully up to the exacting standards of Oisín who had complained to the saint:

> I often slept abroad on the hill,
> Under the grey dew, on the foliage of trees,
> And I was not accustomed to a supperless bed
> While there was a stag on yonder hill!

Patrick replied with justifiable indignation:

> Thou hast not a bed without food,
> Thou gettest seven cakes of bread,
> And a large roll of butter,
> And a quarter of beef every day.

But the hero had known better times:

> I saw a rowan berry
> twice larger than thy roll,
> And I saw an ivy leaf
> Larger and wider than thy cake of bread.
> I saw a quarter of a blackbird
> Which was larger than thy quarter of beef;
> 'Tis it that fills my soul with sadness,
> To be in thy house thou poor wretch!

To prove the point Oisín, accompanied by a guide, set off once more to Glenasmole. There they found still growing a rowan tree with fruits to equal those of bygone days and on a cliff face an ivy bush with immense leaves. They had to go as far as the Curragh of Kildare before they could find a worthy descendant of the great blackbirds. But they caught it with the aid of one of their hounds and brought their trophies back to the saint's household.

Clearly the blackbirds and rowans have become extinct, though whether or not Patrick had a hand in this is uncertain. The saint's way with reptiles and other defenceless animals is only too well known and would not earn him much respect amongst conservationists in our enlightened days. The ivy, as we have seen, lived on. However, it is not fair to give all the blame for faunal extinction to St Patrick. Finn himself had led the way. The 'Finnian Hunt of Sliabh Truim' sets the hero on a trail of destruction:

Of all the Piasts that fell by Fionn
The number never can be told . . . .

He slew the Piast of Loch Neagh
And the monster of Glen-an-smoil

to name but two.

The poems are set out in the *Transactions of the Ossianic Society* published in the 1850s. One more, 'The Adventures of the Omadán Mór' tells of:

A city that shone like unto gold;
There was no colour which eye had seen
That was not in the mansion, and many more . . .

Dun an Oir is its name,
the strong Dun of Glen an Smoil

and the poem goes on to mention that the glen is always full of witchcraft.

And finally, there is the tale of Finn's ransom. His kidnapping did not take place in the Glen but the ransom paid for his release was a living specimen of every species of bird which lived in Ireland. Among them were 'two stonechats from Glenasmole'. Maybe their capture explains the fact that nobody seems to have seen any stonechats there in recent times. This is quite puzzling because the gorse-covered pasture near Glenasmole Lodge looks like an ideal habitat for them.

The Watercourse

A little way down the hill from Finn MacCool's Stone the diverted Dodder, enlarged by its union with the Cot Brook, is confined within the concrete banks and floor of the artificial Watercourse which goes all the way along the left hand side of the upper lake in Glenasmole. Even the concrete can't always stand up to the force of the angry Dodder and great slabs of the bed and walls were torn out at the time of Hurricane Charlie in 1986. But usually the river flows gently over the level bed.

The land on either side is green pasture, growing on the

One of the many waterfalls in the Dodder Gorge.

delta gravel carried down by the streams and deposited where the ground levelled out. Gorse and broom grow by the banks, the gorse beginning to show its yellow flowers as early as January. In May and June the landscape is a riot of golden yellow when both gorse and broom are out. A little later, when the seeds of the broom have ripened, their long black pods split open explosively to scatter the seed: on a calm summer's day the cracking sound disturbs the silence of the hillside.

Farther downstream the Slade Brook joins the Watercourse on the left and the river, now incorporating Dodder, Slade and Cot Brooks, goes on to the 'new' bridge of Castlekelly. Up above the bridge there are pines and larches and a cheerful, noisy rookery. Below it a weir with a concrete sill bars the river's passage down the old bed of the Slade Brook and in normal conditions only a trickle of water makes its way into the reservoir. The Watercourse goes straight ahead under a two-arched stone bridge and flows by the side of the upper lake. From this point for 4 kilometres downstream river, lakes and landscape are the property of the Corporation of Dublin — a sort of extra-territorial extension of the city fathers, surrounded by the County.

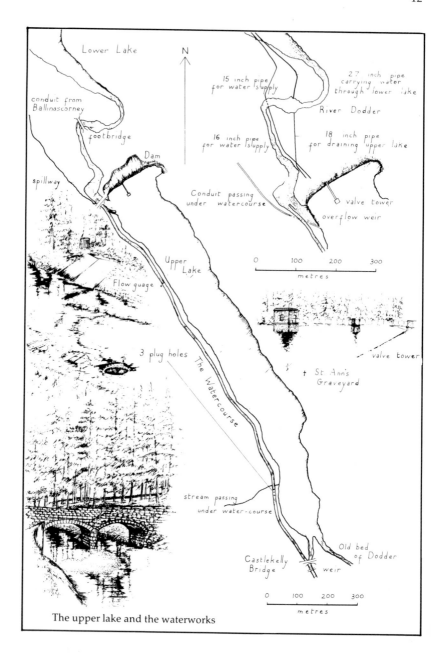

Lower Lake

N

conduit from Ballinascorney

footbridge

Dam

spillway

Upper Lake

Flow guage

3 plug holes

The Watercourse

stream passing under water-course

Castlekelly Bridge

15 inch pipe for water supply

27 inch pipe carrying water through lower lake

River Dodder

16 inch pipe for water supply

18 inch pipe for draining upper lake

Conduit passing under watercourse

valve tower

overflow weir

0   100   200   300
metres

valve tower

✝ St. Ann's Graveyard

Old bed of Dodder

weir

0   100   200   300
metres

The upper lake and the waterworks

CHAPTER 2

Glenasmole — the lakes and waterworks

From Castlekelly Bridge to Fort Bridge, a distance of 4 km, the Dodder flows within the property of Dublin Corporation. Few reaches of the valley could be less urban; the extraterritorial anomaly exists because the land was acquired for the construction of the waterworks. For more than half of this section, the valley is occupied by two man-made lakes. Much of the scenery by the lakes is equally artificial, the result of landscaping in the 19th century. The Dodder and the tributary streams are led over, under and past the lakes so that, quite apart from the peace and beauty of the valley, the exploration of the Watercourse makes a study in itself.

The engineering schemes

Water from the upper valley passes beneath Castlekelly Bridge, the second crossing of the same name: the first spans the abandoned valley of the Dodder up the hill in the village. This one has a plaque on both sides, to commemorate its building in February 1906 to replace the structure destroyed by flood on 25th August the year before. Eighty-one years later to the day the rains associated with Hurricane Charlie failed to carry away the bridge but caused spectacular flooding all the way downstream.

This is the point where the landscape becomes completely dominated by the vision and skill of engineers of the 19th century. They replaced on a smaller scale a lake which had filled the valley at the end of the ice age when the great glacier of the midlands was melting away. But that was thousands of years ago and ever since the Dodder flowed freely and fiercely through the gorge, tearing away its sides of glacial till, carrying immense quantities of gravel to be dumped at Firhouse and beyond and bringing silt all the way to Dublin Bay.

The first proposal for a reservoir in Glenasmole was made in a report to the Drainage Commissioners in 1844 by one of the most distinguished engineers of the time, Robert Mallet. He considered placing a dam in the gorge where the lower lake now lies but dismissed the idea:

> Between these [slopes of the valley] it would be possible to construct a reservoir, covering from 60 to 90 acres; but the situation is far from desirable, and the construction of any reservoir here, which would lay the bases of the impending clay banks under water, would certainly be attended with extensive land-slips, injurious alike to the land above and to the capacity of the basin below; nor could any sufficient area be here conveniently obtained, that would control the waters delivered into it from the great catchment above it.

After considering a number of possible sites higher up the valley, he finally proposed building a dam about 500 metres upstream of the present embankment. This was to be 30 metres high and 312 metres across. The capacity of the reservoir would have been 6 million cubic metres, nearly four times that of the upper lake. The aims of the plan were twofold: to control flooding and to improve the supply to the water mills — domestic water was not a consideration at the time.

The Drainage Commissioners were unimpressed and Mallet again proposed using the Dodder in 1860 when an improved water supply for the city of Dublin was under consideration. His scheme, however, failed because it could not provide enough water for the entire city. The next move came in 1877 when the Rathmines Township Commissioners were exploring the ways and means of supplying their residents with water. They asked Richard Hassard to advise on the feasibility either of a supply from the higher levels of the Grand Canal or from the Dublin Corporation's reservoir at Stillorgan.

In his report Hassard put forward the idea of the two dams in Glenasmole and his plan was adopted with very little alteration. Glenasmole would certainly have been inadequate for the needs of the whole city — so the Corporation had some grounds for rejecting Mallet's plan. But the much smaller project of a supply for Rathmines and Rathgar was quite another matter and so the waterworks we know and love were created. The construction work on the two reservoirs took place from 1883 to 1887. In our journey down the Dodder the highest section of the undertaking has been described in the previous chapter, beginning with the diversion of the Dodder towards the Cot Brook (page 31).

The greater part of the system lies within Glenasmole and most of it can be seen from the left bank where an impressive display of notices greets the unwary visitor. The gist of what they say is that anyone is welcome to visit or to fish — provided they obtain a permit. The said permits are very willingly given by the authorities who are happy to welcome the public to their property but who also want to keep the situation under control. A custodian lives in the cottage just above the bridge. It has been a family occupation for a long, long time and Eddy Costello, the present incumbent, represents the third generation.

Diverting the Dodder

Just upstream of the bridges at Castlekelly the river is diverted to the left by a sill set in the bed of reinforced concrete. In exceptional floods the water can pass over the sill and make its way down a sloping apron of stone into the bed of the Slade Brook and so to the lake. At normal flows all the water from the upper valley passes under the slightly asymmetrical two-arched bridge and makes its way along a channel named by its designers the Artificial Watercourse.

The Watercourse was excavated in the glacial till and lined with rubble set in concrete. The stones of the rubble are local, mainly granite. In dry weather the Dodder trickles gently along, scarcely covering the level paving of the bed. It is a favourite haunt of dippers under these conditions. Moderate floods bring the water close to the top of the masonry lining, a depth of more than 2 metres. The Water-

Larch

course was designed to take the worst floods that the Dodder could muster and nearly always succeeds. Hurricane Charlie in 1986 was only a little too much for it and the sort of rainfall which accompanied the hurricane seldom happens more than once or twice in a hundred years. So the 19th-century engineers may be credited with a sound appraisal of the dangers.

The purpose of the Watercourse is to keep the water of the Dodder out of its natural valley, bypassing the upper lake which is the reservoir for domestic supplies. The reason for this undertaking is that in wet weather the streams from the peaty slopes dissolve humic acids and turn pale brown. This colouring, however pleasing to the nature lover, would have been unacceptable to the residents of Rathmines and Rathgar and the slow sand filtration which was used could not discharge the colour. Nowadays the acids can be precipitated by chemical treatment but the technique had not been sufficiently developed in the 19th century.

Saving the drinking water

The water draining through the lower slopes of Glenasmole, with their underlying slates and volcanic rock and their blanket of glacial till, is quite different in its chemical composition and much more suitable for drinking. This is the water which is collected in the upper lake. The streams of the right bank flow directly into it but those on the left bank have to be led through culverts which pass underneath the Watercourse.

At the upper end of the lake the ground slopes gently so that there is a gradual change from dry land through a swamp, filled with willow thicket and fringed by reeds, to a shallow bay with bullrushes and so to the deeper water. In winter whooper swans visit from time to time, migrants from Iceland distinguished by their lemon yellow bills and loud trumpeting call. Moorhen and dabchick are permanent residents, nesting amongst the reeds. Moorhens are plentiful from this point all the way down the Dodder as far as the tidal water. The dabchicks spend most of their lives in the lake, only occasionally visiting calm stretches in the lower reaches.

A well-maintained gravel footpath runs between the Watercourse and the lake, shaded, wherever there is enough land for them, by mature and stately European larch and Scots pine. The larch has the unusual habit for conifers of shedding all its leaves in winter and leaving the branches bare except for the lines of little oval cones which stand out on the twigs. In spring new green cones develop, at first bearing minute pink flowers. Then pale green leaves clothe the branches, in autumn turning to a marvellous golden colour. Scots pine once was a native Irish tree but became very rare and perhaps extinct. It was reintroduced in the 17th century and quickly became one of the most popular trees in forestry planting. The European larch was first planted in Ireland in or about 1740.

One hundred paces downstream of the beginning of the pines and larches on the left you can see, in dry weather, three round openings on the bed of the Watercourse. Sometimes they are closed by wooden covers, sometimes left open so that the water flows through them down into the upper lake. When the flow off the peatlands is slow, the brown colouring is scarcely visible and the water can be used for the domestic supply — in such times of drought the supply from the smaller, peat-free catchment can be too low and therefore the supplement is especially valuable.

A little farther downstream and still on the left, a rivulet on the hillside plunges steeply downhill over a rocky bed and disappears into the ground on the far side of the water-course. This is the first of the underpassing rivers which goes beneath the channel and under the path. It enters the upper lake beside an ash tree. Each of these streams has a grit trap so that the sand and silt which they carry is kept out of the reservoir.

Across the lake the glacial till blanket lies unevenly over the hill slopes. The lower parts are mainly green pasture, with grazing cattle. Higher up, bracken takes over in places. The path of the tributary streams can be traced by the hazel and alder bushes which shade them. St Ann's graveyard is low on the hillside a little way above the lake, and higher up the hill is the hamlet of the same name.

Alder

The roots of the mountains

The underlying rock of the same steep slope is slate to the left, schist to the right. The junction can't be seen because it is deeply buried by the glacial till. Farther to the right the hills are purplish brown rather than green: heather moorland as opposed to pasture. The heather lies on the granite, the pasture on schist and slate. The slate to the left was formed before the Caledonian folding which built the Wicklow Mountains.

There was an ocean at that time, some 450 million years ago, to the north and west of a line from Clogherhead to Nenagh. This ocean was squeezed out of existence as two continental plates drifted together while the present day Atlantic formed. Ultimately the northwest portion of Ireland was forced up against the southwest, folding the rock and bringing about the conditions which caused molten granite to be forced up as a dome deep beneath the older rock. This granite is dated to 404 million years ago, give or take 24 million. Around the edges of the dome the old slates were roasted and recrystallized to form schist, a shining flaky rock.

The important point about schist is that it is much more resistant to erosion than either granite or slate and wherever it appears the mountain scenery is more dramatic than that underlain by the granite. In this case, before the ice age, the ancestral Dodder had made itself a broad valley in the relatively soft granite but was unable to erode the schist to the same extent. Therefore the river could do little more than cut downwards and hence the gorge of Glenasmole, so different from the gentle slopes higher up Kippure. The narrowness of Glenasmole made the building of the dams and the creation of the lakes feasible.

After the larches the Watercourse enters a series of 3 concrete-lined tunnels, bordered by a neatly-built stone wall. The tunnels run, with occasional openings to the surface, for 130 metres. Nobody now knows why this portion had to be covered over. In very high floods the tunnels cause serious trouble because tree trunks and other objects — even a drowned deer in 1986 — block the openings.

The gauging weir

Downstream of the three tunnels, the Watercourse takes a lazy S-bend. Where it straightens out, the bed is paved and for a short section the banks on either side are covered by smooth concrete. On the left bank just upstream of this section there is a little kiosk and opposite to it a measuring board. This is all part of a gauging weir and very much more complicated than it looks. The upstream sides of the concrete walls are curved, constricting the flow a little. Then the walls run parallel and finally they diverge. When there is a good flow in progress, the surface upstream is held at a high level, then it bends downwards and the water flows smoothly between the parallel walls. The divergence of the walls causes turbulence and the level rises again.

Using a flow meter the speed of the water passing between the parallel walls can be measured accurately for varying levels of the surface just upstream. From these measurements a calibration curve is calculated. Once this has been done, all that is needed to gauge the flow is to measure the depth of water. The measuring board is

The gauging weir

marked with lines numbered from 1 to 7. The distance between them seems to correspond to no known unit of length but actually shows the depth of the water in feet. The kiosk contains an automatic recording depth gauge. At low flows a small pipe can be seen below it on the bed of the Watercourse. This is the entrance to a vertical pipe containing the float which operates the depth gauge.

After the flow gauge comes another of the underpassing streams, going down the hillside by a series of steps. In 1991 it was overflowing into the Watercourse because the culvert had become choked with sand over the years and was awaiting a major scouring operation. One more stream, the biggest and the most remarkable, enters the lake, flowing between a narrow pair of stone walls and over a stone apron. It appears suddenly on the right hand side of the path, where the larch trees end and a laurel hedge begins. The opening to the culvert lies just beyond the bridge over the Watercourse and has a V-weir to measure the flow. The water is crystal clear and comes from two sources. These, the Ballinascorney and Ballymaice Streams, lie further down the valley, the latter at a distance of 3 km.

The Piperstown Stream

There once was a third supply to the Ballinascorney Culvert but it became a casualty of war. During the Second World War there was a severe shortage of engineering and building materials, in particular of large diameter pipes for water mains. The Piperstown Stream, from the right bank, had been brought to join the culvert by a 24-inch pipe which led it *under* the lower lake and up on the other side. This pipe was excavated and used to lay a large main in Benburb Street. It was replaced by a 9-inch pipe directly connected into the 15-inch main which leads to Ballyboden.

The embankment

The dam at the end of the lake has a lovely steep grassy bank, maintained by mowing at intervals and steep enough to encourage small people to roll down it. It looks a simple enough structure but in fact represents a considerable feat in engineering because, in the words of Arthur Tyrrell, writing in 1888:

> . . . there occurred on the eastern side of the valley veins and deposits of sand and gravel, extending for a considerable distance into the hill, and rendering it necessary to follow them in by headings driven down one over another and filled with concrete, the ground being too steep for open trenches. This operation was one of considerable difficulty, owing to the loose nature of the sand and the quantity of spring water met with. The lower heading at the upper embankment was extended 120 feet into the hillside, until the deposit of sand had been completely cut through and a wall of hard blue clay reached. Into this clay the heading was carried sufficiently far to ensure a sound junction being effected between the concrete filling and the impervious material at its termination. From the floor of the lower heading a trench was then sunk to a depth of 32 feet, when the hard clay was reached; and the whole was refilled with carefully rammed concrete. After this the next heading was proceeded with, and filled up with concrete in the same manner; and so on until a height of 84 feet from the bottom was attained, when the work was completed by a short length of open trench. The headings being only 5 feet in height and all heavily timbered, this part of the work was necessarily very slow and tedious, greatly retarding the progress of the upper reservoir embankment, and consequently the final completion of the works. The upper reservoir has an area of 57 acres and contains 357,000,000 gallons, its embankment being 70 feet in height at the deepest part.

The upper lake

In metric terms the lake holds, or held then, 1.6 million cubic metres and had a surface of 23 hectares. In the course of one hundred years both its volume and area have been reduced by siltation, to some degree by the deposition of the same sort of gravel which coated the clay of the glacial till and gave the 19th-century engineers so much trouble.

At the near end of the dam, landscape gardening of the last century begins to make its appearance, with clusters of rhododendrons and laurel. On the eastern side of the Watercourse the lake meets a concrete weir, 200 feet long, over which the water escapes in very wet weather. Its considerable length was deemed necessary by the engineers to cope with the worst floods.

About one third of the way along the dam an iron bridge leads out to the neat valve house built of granite blocks. It stands on top of a tower more than 70 feet high with three openings at different levels. These allow water to flow from the lake into the water supply pipe at the bottom. Also at the bottom of the tower is a bigger pipe which can be used to empty the reservoir and a second, smaller, emptying pipe which discharges into the lower lake.

The view from the centre of the dam is up towards Kippure with its heather moor and the gorge of the upper Dodder. Below lie the pasture and farms whose farthest extent marks the line where glacial till carried down from the north covered the local granite. Downstream of the embankment you can get an impression of the appearance of Glenasmole before the lakes were created: a splendid steep-sided valley with a flat bed. Larch and Scots pine are the most plentiful trees, but there are birch, beech and ash as well and, in summer, a big clump of the pink-flowered rose-bay willow herb, a flower generally considered to have escaped from cottage gardens.

The valve house

The spillway

Opposite the dam, a stone bridge supported by iron girders and one central pier spans the Watercourse. Just below the bridge the stream heads for the spillway, a magnificent artificial cascade which brings it down to the floor of the valley in the direction of the lower lake. At the top of the spillway the Watercourse makes a right-angled turn and the water is led through a curious stone structure. It is a long weir pierced by twenty rectangular openings, each made from two upright blocks of granite crossed by a lintel. Its purpose puzzled even his professional colleagues when Arthur Tyrrell presented a paper on the works to the Institute of Mechanical Engineers in 1888. He explained it thus:

> The object [of the weir] was in times of heavy flood to prevent the great body of water impinging on the side walls of the tumbling bay, in consequence of the direction of the current being suddenly turned at right angles, and to check the rush and swirl of water which at such times would otherwise have taken place in the diverted channel at the point of its junction with the tumbling bays and by-wash. This precautionary work had entirely answered its purpose. The twenty culverts through the weir were of sufficient discharging capacity to carry off not only the ordinary flow of the river, but even considerable floods; while at times of excessive rainfall, when the diverted channel was running nearly full, the surplus water passed quietly over the crest of the weir, leaving comparatively still water behind it, the velocity of the water in the channel being no greater at this point than in any other part of the artificial watercourse.

The 'tumbling bay' is contained by a gentle, curved slope paved with granite. As the water seldom covers this slope, it has developed a pleasing flora of ferns, grasses and herb robert. The view down the cascade and across the valley is of a forest of stately pine trees and larches climbing the steep slope opposite. Rhododendrons grow on both sides.

The spillway is a great series of five slopes separated by levels. It always looks impressive, but deserves a special visit after a few days' heavy rain when the entire channel is filled from bank to bank with roaring, foaming water — and you can see how well the design has stood the test of time.

Sad to say, recent developments in assessing the safety of dams have questioned the capacity of the cascade. The dams in Glenasmole are classed as Category A — this implies that their destruction would lead to loss of life. Accordingly precautions must be taken to ensure that they can survive floods which are so rare that they may never have been recorded. The works in Glenasmole did stand up to the rainfall of Hurricane Charlie — but the engineers have to accept that worse could happen. If the cascade were to fail to take the entire flood, water would cross the embankment and could tear it to pieces. So the bridge over the Watercourse and the cascade itself will have to be enlarged.

This will all entail major development work — a challenging project for the engineers involved. The cheapest and easiest way would doubtless be to dig where necessary and coat everything with concrete. The greatest part of the challenge lies in the ability of the designers to create something with the beauty of the stonework of the 19th-century structures.

The woodland

The footpath after passing the head of the waterfall winds its way gently down the slope beneath the trees. The steep banks to the left are deeply shaded and often damp with percolating water. These are the conditions that ferns need and there is a fantastic natural fernery on the slopes wherever these have not been invaded by the rhododendrons. Innocent day-trippers admire the rhododendrons at all times of the year, but above all in spring when sombre green is covered with purple flowers.

You must not even whisper your love of rhododendrons to earnest naturalists. The problem is that, although rhododendrons once were native Irish plants, they have been extinct since before the last glaciation and were reintroduced by landscape gardeners. The purple-flowered species *Rhododendron ponticum* thrives on acid soils. It is so vigorous that it can cover great areas of hillside, smothering just about everything else. Because it casts a dense shade winter and summer no other plants and very few animals can live with it, so the rhododendron hillsides are nice to see from a distance but very dull to walk through.

Happily, in Glenasmole, they have not succeeded in taking over the hillside and the ferns survive. One of the best and certainly the most convenient displays is on a steep bank to the left of the path. Two species are dominant: male fern and *Polystichum setiferum*. The English name of the latter is 'soft prickly shield fern' and this is a case where the Latin is easier to remember. Both look very much alike, with big fronds, often one metre in length and growing in lovely big tufts. The fronds of polystichum often wither and disappear in winter, but male fern stays the whole year round; its smallest leaflets have soft tips while polystichum is slightly prickly. Other ferns on the bank are hart's tongue, broad buckler fern and lady fern. Neither male fern nor lady fern have any relationship nor, indeed, any sex. The names probably contrast the rugged and delicate appearances of the two.

With the ferns grow wild strawberries, herb robert and the golden saxifrage whose tiny yellow flowers are amongst the earliest to brighten the roadsides in spring. Ivy climbs up the old trees. This high-climbing ivy is, by European standards, a rare plant. Ivy in most countries stays on the floor of the forests but in Ireland because there is so little frost it is able to survive in much more exposed places. Controversy on whether it damages trees or not will probably never end. A luxuriant growth of ivy often

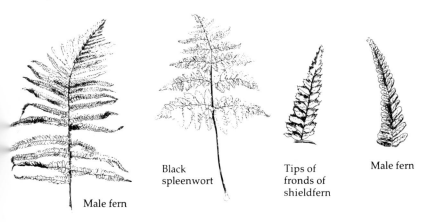

Male fern

Black
spleenwort

Tips of
fronds of
shieldfern

Male fern

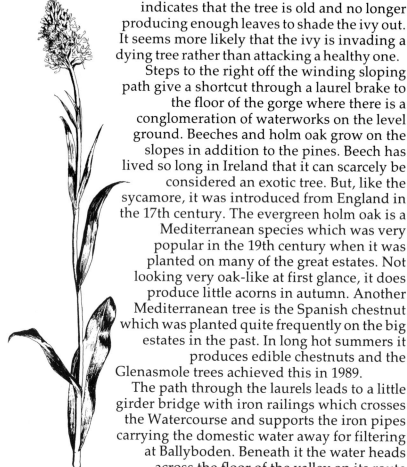

Spotted orchid

indicates that the tree is old and no longer producing enough leaves to shade the ivy out. It seems more likely that the ivy is invading a dying tree rather than attacking a healthy one.

Steps to the right off the winding sloping path give a shortcut through a laurel brake to the floor of the gorge where there is a conglomeration of waterworks on the level ground. Beeches and holm oak grow on the slopes in addition to the pines. Beech has lived so long in Ireland that it can scarcely be considered an exotic tree. But, like the sycamore, it was introduced from England in the 17th century. The evergreen holm oak is a Mediterranean species which was very popular in the 19th century when it was planted on many of the great estates. Not looking very oak-like at first glance, it does produce little acorns in autumn. Another Mediterranean tree is the Spanish chestnut which was planted quite frequently on the big estates in the past. In long hot summers it produces edible chestnuts and the Glenasmole trees achieved this in 1989.

The path through the laurels leads to a little girder bridge with iron railings which crosses the Watercourse and supports the iron pipes carrying the domestic water away for filtering at Ballyboden. Beneath it the water heads across the floor of the valley on its route towards the old bed of the Dodder and so to the lower lake. After crossing the bridge you can walk back along the edge of the Watercourse towards the foot of the embankment. On the left you pass the Glenasmole rain gauge from which daily measurements have been recorded since 1883, including one of 182.5 mm for the 24 hour period beginning at 9.00 am on 25th August 1986.

The big birch tree near the rain gauge has a witch's broom amongst its lower branches. This mass of twigs, looking like a bird's nest, is an abnormal growth caused by a species of mite.

Pipes and traps

At the foot of the cascade, the Ordovician strata are exposed, greenish slaty rock in steeply dipping, nearly vertical beds. The rock is formed from sediments which, more than 440 million years ago, were deposited in a situation similar to that of Dublin Bay. A great river carried slightly muddy silt down to the sea where it settled on the bed. The river flowed over an even older landscape, of a period represented now by the rocks of Howth and Bray Head. Originally the beds of sediment lay horizontally, and solidified in that position. Then the movement of the continental plates compressed them into a series of folds, with the granite mass which forms the Wicklow Mountains as a core.

At the base of the embankment a stone-faced tunnel, with a locked iron gate, leads mysteriously into darkness. It was an 'eduction tunnel', constructed before the dam and serving to carry the water of the Dodder away while the dam and the watercourse were being built. The eduction tunnel remained open until the dam was completed. The final and decisive act in making the lake was the plugging of this tunnel with bricks and mortar.

The three great iron pipes from the lake lie in the tunnel and then bend downwards to go underground for a while. The enormous pipe on the right hand side, 24 inches (61cm) diameter, and the next, 18 inches, are for draining the lake should this ever be necessary. The third pipe, 16 inches, carries the water supply. Their route below the ground can be traced by the valves on the surface, protected by concrete cylinders.

In the middle of the lowest pool of the cascade, a little concrete dome hides the entrance to a 24-inch iron pipe. A second pipe leaves the pool just below the wall on the right bank. Both lead to the valve house beside the cascade and then run underground to enter a pair of concrete troughs, each divided into three by partitions. These are grit traps, to collect the gravel brought down by floods. The pairing arrangement allows for accidents or for closing down one or other for maintenance.

Water passes through either or both of these to an open culvert and then to a functional-looking house of concrete, in sad contrast to the lovely stonework of most of the 19th-century buildings. This is a screen chamber where floating debris — which passes over the silt trap — is collected. From the screen chamber the water goes down into a 27-inch pipe through which it flows underneath the lower lake to discharge into the Dodder beyond its dam. This pipe, bypassing the lower lake, can carry 2.4 million gallons a day, the minimum requirements of the millers in the 19th century. The water which flowed above ground in the river bed filled the lower lake for a reserve. In times of drought water from the upper lake could be brought into the millers' supply through the silt trap. Although the scheme in its final form was designed for domestic water, the law required that the millers would have first preference.

As there are no more millers, the flow in the Dodder is maintained more to take care of the fish than for any other purpose nowadays. However, the control system continues to be very important in times of flood. When heavy rains threaten, as much water as possible is allowed to bypass the lower lake which can then be used to hold back some of the flood water and also reduce the threat to the dam itself.

The lower lake

On the other side of the little iron footbridge, with its white-painted railings, the path continues down the hill, passing the Superintendent's House: a delightful stone building with brick borders to doors and windows, slate roof and decorated woodwork beneath the eaves. Dry rot and decay and dreadful redesigning of the house led to a very successful refurbishing completed in 1989. In the course of the work, partitions and a false ceiling were removed from the front room which was originally a large hall with a beautiful wooden roof. This has been restored and the hall may be used in the future as an information centre. Much too big to have been part of the superintendent's residence, it may have been a board room for the Commissioners.

The atmosphere of this part of the Waterworks property belongs to another age. The old house blends perfectly with the tall pines and other trees which seem to have lived there since the beginning of time — rather than since the Commissioners ordered good landscaping a hundred and twenty years ago. There still is a stable where Neddy, the last horse to work for the Corporation, dwelt in honourable retirement until 1987. Red squirrels live here, supplementing their natural diet with foraging trips to steal the food which belongs to the superintendent's hens: lovely hens which range freely in and around a traditional hen run.

The path from the house leads along to the edge of the lower lake. Beside it, to the left, the pair of iron pipes with the water for Ballyboden run at the bottom of the bank: sometimes exposed, sometimes hidden in concrete and sometimes buried.

The upper end of the lower lake is a wonderful reed swamp with purple loosestrife and a profusion of willows. On the steep bank across the lake birch and hazel are plentiful, taking over from pine and larch. Surprisingly, they are the only native species of tree which are abundant in the valley. Oak is positively rare, ash and mountain ash are thinly scattered and the woodland around the lakes is almost entirely a planted one. In places the cliff is vertical and bare of plant life, revealing the grey clays of the glacial till.

The shrubs growing by the fence beside the road along the lower lake include Japanese knot-grass, distinguished by its big leaves which are cut off square at the base. It was brought to Europe about the middle of the 19th century and planted on the great estates to form ground cover for such birds as pheasant and woodcock.

Moorhens live permanently by the lake and a number of water birds visit it. Sometimes teal go there in winter while all the year round several species of gull rest on the water. Herring gull are the most plentiful: with the great black-backed gulls they gather to forage on the rubbish tip nearby. Black-headed gulls also visit the lake and lesser black-backed gulls come early in spring and stay around for the summer.

The lower lake ends in an embankment, concrete sill and valve house very similar to those of the upper. The overflow goes through a pair of stone arches and down another great spillway. The 27-inch pipe which runs along the bed of the lake joins with an outlet pipe at the base of the lower valve tower and, together with a 24-inch pipe, brings the water below the dam to the 'millers' gauge'. This is a rectangular pond of stone with a horizontal sill at its downstream edge where the depth of an even flow could be measured. The millers could thereby ensure that they were not being cheated by the domestic users. The gauge effectively marks the end of the waterworks. From this point the Dodder flows once again in the channel which it excavated for itself.

Larch and pine grow on the slopes to the right of the dam; beeches and ash make a grove on the hillside at the other end. From the path on the left bank of the lower lake the valley has a very closed-in feeling. The cliff looms above the water, its little forest of hazel and birch going all the way to the skyline which is broken at just one point by a small building, marked on the large scale map as a Water Tower. It marks the spot where the Piperstown Stream was swallowed up by the 24-inch main and brought beneath the lower lake. Now the stream goes to a mere 9-inch pipe which is laid laid across the top of the dam of the lower lake to reach the Ballyboden main.

The cliff is more than 30 metres high, reaching the 200 metre contour. Above that level the slope of the hill is much more gentle, rising gradually over Piperstown to the Hellfire Club — but all these are hidden. On the left hand side of the valley the hills are higher, but not nearly as steep and the view across the embankment from the right bank of the lower lake is of a long line of hills. They seem to be of equal height but are actually climbing gently as you go up the valley. Slievenabawnoge, (*the hill of the litle enclosure*) is the first, with a portion of forestry plantation: pines, with larch below. Water from the great glacial lake which once filled the valley flowed out first to the left and later to the right of the summit of Slievenabawnoge.

The stone of Slievenabawnoge is mainly dolerite, a bluish igneous rock which forced its way into the older slates but never got to the surface to make a lava flow. It was formed some time before the Wicklow granite but still was part of the great Caledonian earth movements. The next hill, Ballymorefinn, (*the great town of Finn*) marks the south-eastern extremity of the igneous rock and beyond it the hilltops, as well as their flanks, are slaty for a short way, then schist and, finally, granite on Corrig Mountain.

The mountain road which serves the houses runs between the 213 and 274 metre (700 and 900 foot) contours and lies a little below the highest level of the glacial till. The road peaks at 253 metres in the townland of Allagour, (*the goat's cliff*). Below the road is steep sloping pasture, divided by hedges. The higher ground is mostly bracken-covered and above that has the blue-green look of heather moorland. To the right of Slievenabawnoge the hills in the townland of Ballymaice are green pasture to the top, divided all the way by old hedges. The underlying rock is slate, buried beneath the glacial till. Before continuing the journey down the Dodder we must pause to go by the other side of the upper lake.

The right bank of the upper lake

The walk along the left banks of both lakes follows smooth gravel paths and, in places, tarmac roads. This is essential as a service road for the waterworks and, as a bonus, provides easy access for visitors. The right bank is a different world, a wild place where a narrow path wanders between trees and bushes. Access from Castlekelly Bridge is by a white gate a little way up the road leading to a lane, shaded by old larch trees.

The lane crosses, by a stone bridge, a small stream which makes its way discreetly through a swamp before entering the lake and joining once more with the separated waters. There are beds of fool's watercress, a rather uneatable plant with pointed, not rounded leaves. Kingfishers visit the stream and the swamp from time to time, the willows and alders providing them with plenty of the low perches over the water which they need.

This little stream is all that is left of the main Dodder since its diversion towards the Cot Brook. It is a lovely, gurgling stream with clear water splashing over a bed of clean gravel. On its right bank, about half way between the

Monkey flower

lake and the hamlet of Cunard on the hillside, the stream flows beneath an exposure of grey glutinous mud. This has been identified as a lake bed deposit. At one time it was possible to see that the mud had been formed in layers, each layer or 'varve' formed in the course of a year. Sixty of these in all were counted, suggesting that the lake existed for sixty years before the ice dam melted and let all the water escape through the river valley.

On gravel banks in the bed of the stream in late summer the yellow, bell-shaped flowers of the monkey flower are in bloom. It is a North American species, popular as a garden plant in the 19th century. The first monkey flowers were planted in a garden in Glenasmole about forty years before Nathaniel Colgan completed his survey of wild flowers in 1904. By his time the species had spread far down the Dodder and now it is one of the river's most characteristic wild plants.

Reed mace, the tall rush-like plant with big brown flowering heads like furry sausages, grows in the swamp and in patches by the lake margin all the way along. Willows are the dominant tree, mostly the native sally with its small leaves. Those with long, narrow, typically willow-shaped leaves are osiers. Horsetails and purple loosestrife also share the swamp.

After the swamp, the path runs along beside hedges of blackthorn with willow, ash and hawthorn. The steep slopes on the right are clothed with glacial till: a very uneven covering, with hummocks and knolls. As a glaciated landscape these slopes are particularly interesting because the till is many thousands of years older than the deposits of the lower Dodder valley. The ice fields reached their greatest extent over Ireland in the Munsterian phase — the name is not an obscure Germano-scientific term but simply means that the ice extended to the province of Munster. Deposits from the Munsterian glacier can, according to Francis Synge, be traced as high as 360 metres on Kippure. This cold period ended 130,000 years ago and a mild 'inter-glacial' phase persisted for 65,000 years after which the last cold phase took place.

The steepest banks can only just about support their covering of grass and are being worn away by a combination of grazing and rainfall. Old accounts of the Dodder mention the frequency of landslides on the steeper slopes. The green pasture is cut off from the waterworks property by an elderly chain-link fence, punctuated from time to time by neat gateways, the gates supported by cylindrical piers built of granite, surmounted by low conical caps.

In places by the lake the giant horsetail, with its almost cream-coloured stems, grows. Other horsetails are plentiful in the damp places but this, the most spectacular of them, is not quite so common. Together with the ferns, horsetails are the latter day representatives of plants which dominated the surface of the earth before the flowering plants had evolved.

St Ann's

About 600 paces down the path, paces which can be uncommonly slithery in wet weather since a herd of cows claim prior rights, there is a decrepit iron gate supported at one end by one of the waterworks stone gate piers and at the other by a concrete post. A path leads up the hill from this, through a narrow track in a jungle of blackthorn to the pasture up above. A short climb then leads to St Ann's churchyard.

St Ann came to the district by etymological accident. A rather unknown bishop called Sanctan or Sentan is commemorated and Sentan's Church was corrupted to that of Saint Ann. The Book of Leinster refers to him as Sentan, son of the king of Britain. Some centuries later, the Annals of the Four Masters record the death of an Abbot of the Church of Bishop Sanctan in 952. Nearly four hundred years after that, in 1326, the district was described as 'lying within the Irishry, therefore, waste and unprofitable' — one of countless cases where the settlers showed their ignorance of soil science by blaming the natives for the barren state of mountain land. The church continued in use for another two centuries.

Its remnants stand within the stone boundary wall of the cemetery and at the gate there is a granite font, its undoubted antiquity equalled only by the uncertainty of its date. The most interesting monument is a large 19th-century tomb with the names of Maurice Collins and some fellow members of a remarkable community. At Ann

Mount, a nearby house leased from the landowner Charles Cobbe, Maurice Collins and John Stewart founded a monastery in 1821. They were members of the third order of Carmel and for many years ran a school for the local children, a school supported entirely by voluntary subscriptions.

Maurice Collins served as prior until his death in 1865 at the age of 94. John Stewart subsequently became prior and died in 1887 aged 93. There must be something particularly healthy about the air of Glenasmole. The friars set up their establishment in the first place to bring education to the valley and the school continued for many years. However, the community seems also to have been a cheerfully outgoing and hospitable group and the monastery became a fashionable place to go for a Sunday afternoon.

William Handcock gives a first-hand account of the monastery and its devotees in the 1870s:

> A mile beyond Friarstown, we come to the well-known Monastery of St. Anne's. A few monks reside here, who hospitably entertain all who come, provided they bring their own provisions, or order them beforehand. Here, during the summer, and sometimes in winter, a quoit club, so called, meets occasionally. Several of its members are more famous for their musical, facetious, or gastronomic, than for their athletic, achievements. The willing monks supply room, fuel and water, and many a pleasant evening is thus spent in the pure air of the mountains.

The great glacial lake

A little way to the north of the hamlet of St Ann's a mound of morainic material marks the spot where the southwards-flowing Midlandian ice field came to a halt. Although the ice extended well to the south of Glenasmole on both sides of the Wicklow Mountains, it failed to force itself all the way up the narrow valley. But it did serve as a natural dam and impounded an enormous lake which stretched all the way back to the slopes of Kippure. The edge of the ice field curved northwards to skirt Slievenabawnoge whose summit stood out above it. The ice reached a height of 370 metres on the edge of Slievenabawnoge and the water

— DODDER SCENES —

TOP: A gully near the summit of Kippure where the infant Dodder has cut its way down through the peat to the underlying gravel.
ABOVE: Peat hag on Kippure near the source of the Dodder.

TOP: Mareen's Brook, one of the highest tributaries of the Dodder.

ABOVE: Frochans grow amongst the heather on the highest reaches of the river.

LEFT: Ice-deposited stones in the stream bed near Glenasmole Lodge: granite surrounding a single piece of porphyry.

OPPOSITE: The water of Mareen's Brook splashing over moss-covered granite boulders.

ABOVE: St Ann's
graveyard, the upper lake
and the lower slopes of
Ballymorefinn.

OPPOSITE TOP: Kippure and
Ballymorefinn from the
road northwest of
St Ann's. The green knoll
in the foreground marks
the moraine deposited by
the northward-moving
Midlandian ice.

OPPOSITE BOTTOM:
An 18th-century
memorial in the old
churchyard at St Ann's.

TOP: Willow and alders growing on the gravel banks downstream of Oldbawn.
ABOVE: The sand-martin cliff.

TOP: Oldbawn Bridge and weir.
ABOVE: The gorge of Mareen's Brook, slopes covered by heather and bracken.
OVERLEAF: Foxgloves growing by the canal diverting the Dodder to the Cot Brook.

leaving the lake cut its way down to flow westwards just below the summit.

As the ice melted away, the level of the lake dropped. The water abandoned the outlet channel to the south of Slievenabawnoge and flowed instead to the north of the mountain and away through Ballinascorney Gap. Finally, as the level continued to fall, the water escaped eastwards through the Piperstown Gap. There are no traces of the shoreline of the lake: they have all been washed away by rain or hidden by landslides.

Back to modern times and continuing the walk along the lane on the north shore of the present lake, there is a wooden shelter after which larches line the banks and the pathway gets more and more shady, the bushes meeting above it. Many woodland plants appear here: the white flowers of wood anemone and wood sorrel are abundant in spring. In summer the tall, drooping grass *Bromus ramosus* flowers together with *Brachypodium sylvaticum*, which forms dense tufts with broad, dark yellow-green leaves. Beech trees and Scots pine grow near the dam around the little bay where the path crosses a tributary stream by an embankment. Close to the dam there is a guelder rose, a rather uncommon and very attractive hedgerow shrub which produces big white flower clusters in summer, and in autumn red shiny berries while the leaves turn a lovely bronze-red colour.

The steep slopes on the right bank above the lower lake, with their birch and hazel woodland, are officially listed as an area of 'National Importance' in the Foras Forbartha book of *Areas of Scientific Interest in Ireland*. Hazel woodland of this kind is seldom left alone to develop fully in the absence of grazing animals. Badgers and foxes live there too. Those who seek comfort rather than a botanically uplifting scramble, however, should cross the dam and continue the journey on the left bank, admiring the hazel from a distance.

Back to the river

Part of the road along the floor of the valley runs along a causeway, between swamps where horsetails grow. This swamp is the remains of an oxbow lake where a meander to the left was cut off at its base when the river took a short cut during a high flood. The tiny, bow-shaped lake has gradually silted up to form a swamp and will eventually emerge as dry land.

At one stage of its career the Dodder flowed at a slightly higher level and swung to the left, cutting away the bank at the far side of the damp fields. The old floodplain, abandoned by the river, is grazed within the farm fence to the left but taken over by thicket on the right. Hazel is the dominant plant here, brightening the scene even before New Year's Day when the earliest of the long, dangling catkins burst out and display their lovely pale yellow-green colour. By February the whole thicket has a look of spring, even though the leaves will not develop for a couple of months.

Alder grows in the damper parts of the thicket and there are occasional bushes of the much rarer spindle tree. One of them stands beside an abandoned white-painted mobile home on the right. From autumn to midwinter it displays little pink berries.

Downstream of the spindle tree, a track to the right leads to a bend in the river where the left bank is heaped with stones, washed out of the glacial till. Many of the stones are

The upper lake.

large ones, up to 60 cm across. All the local rock types are represented: the blue dolerite, greenish slates, plenty of granite and some quartz and a little grey limestone. Very large granite boulders stand out in the stream. They were brought tumbling down the river in high floods in contrast to the other rocks which were carried up the valley by the great glacier.

The valley grows wider, passing a delightfully traditional-looking farm with a neat two-storey dwelling. At the next point on the river limestone pebbles are much more plentiful and before long they outnumber all the other types of rock in the river bed.

Old pine trees shade the gate lodge at the entrance to the Waterworks property. A little way down the road from the gate there is a steep muddy path, between great clumps of blackberries, down to the river which is usually shallow enough to cross by stepping stones. There is something of a path upstream through a thicket of willows, hazel and alder, rich with birdlife especially in spring. At the end of March chiffchaffs make their presence known by their two-noted song and, a little later, the willow warblers arrive. They have the most elegant of bird-songs, a perfect descending cadence of rich notes.

The path ends in a barbed wire fence and from this you can make your way downstream again, climbing for variety to the top of the grassy slopes covering the rubbish tip. Cows graze there and pipes at intervals release the gases from the rubbish. The tip fills Friarstown Glen which I can remember as a pleasant, though faintly impenetrable, thicket similar to the one on the main Dodder.

The bank at the edge of the rubbish tip is stony, perhaps with not quite enough soil to allow grass to cover it. One of the most interesting plants there is coltsfoot which thrives in stony places. Early in spring its yellow flowers sprout from the ground all on their own. The leaves appear later in the season. Another unusual flower is yellow wort, a delicate gentian described in ringing botanical terms as 'glaucous; cauline leaves connate in pairs'. Glaucous refers to the blue-green colour of the leaves; cauline indicates that they grow on the stem but the connate is the most interesting. It means that after beginning to develop separately, the edges of the pairs of leaves fuse together so that the stem appears to be growing up through a series of single, almost circular leaves. It is a beautiful little flower anyway and one which is confined to places where limestone is plentiful.

The glen had once known better things than rubbish. The name of the townland refers to the Friars Minor of Dublin who held land there until the Dissolution. At the end of the 18th century Ponsonby Shaw, a brother of Sir Robert of Bushy Park, indulged in landscaping on a grand scale with grottoes, walks and waterfalls. Unfortunately he included an artificial lake, held by a dam about 13 metres high. It did not last long. And the flood which carried it away removed most of the landscaping too.

The gold rush

From the slopes there is a pleasant view down over the river, and away over the western suburbs to the Fifteen Acres of Phoenix Park and far away to Slieve Gullion. Closer to hand the river runs over a gravel bed — there is gold in that thar gravel and a party of enthusiastic geologists went panning for it in 1986. The lucky members of the prospecting team found some, too: tiny flakes of gold dust that had to be attached to sellotape so that they wouldn't be lost. If you want to join the gold rush you must write away for a prospecting licence. But you might first consider the likelihood of not even earning the price of the stamp as a reward for many hours of heavy work. The latest group of prospectors found that the cost of the beer required to restore them greatly exceeded the value of the gold they won.

It would be more profitable simply to continue a gentle walk down the Dodder having first stopped to clamber about and admire the rock and concrete of the waterfall at Fort Bridge.

CHAPTER 3

Fort Bridge to Templeogue —
through green pasture

The Dodder descends gently in the course of a little more than 6 km in this chapter, with weirs at Firhouse and Templeogue. The 122 metre (400 feet) contour crosses the river very close to Fort Bridge while Templeogue Bridge is 61 metres above sea level. For the first 2 km, to Oldbawn Bridge, the land on the left bank is still occupied by large, old farmsteads. On the right bank bungalows and pitch and putt are beginning to encroach, and there are small factories. The left bank for the next reach, from Oldbawn to Firhouse, is almost entirely parkland, backed by suburbia while the right bank in the course of 1989 suddenly became a built-up area over most of its length — with the important exception of a strip of linear park preserved by the County Council. The third stretch, from Firhouse to Templeogue gradually enters the long-established suburbs of Dublin, but on both sides great expanses of green fields have been preserved.

Dá Dearga's Hostel

At Bohernabreena the road to Ballinascorney Gap is constricted by the sides of the valley and has to make a tight S-bend over Fort Bridge. Bohernabreena commemorates iron age traditions. James Hegarty describes the use of the *bruidhne* of the name and tells the ancient tale of the Destruction of the Bruidhean Dá Derga:

> In ancient times there were, scattered over Ireland, houses of entertainment called Bruidhne, where the traveller might partake freely of food and drink supplied by the owner, the Brughfer. To enable the Brughfer to carry out his

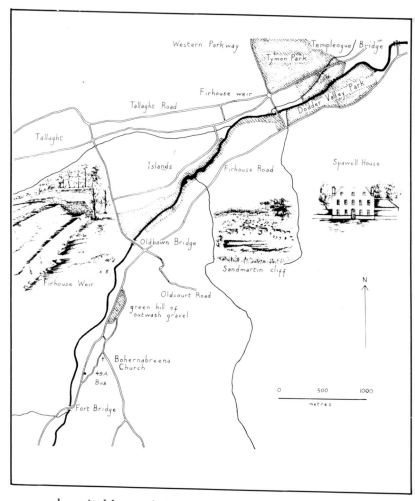

hospitable work he was allowed, by Brehon laws, 1,000 acres of arable land free of rent. There were no fewer than 93 Bruidhne in Leinster alone; from one cause or another the number gradually decreased until about the last century of the pagan era there were but six in all Ireland, of which three were in Leinster — one at Bohernabreena, (Bóthar na bruidhne), one at Lusk, and one in Westmeath. Each Bruidhean had, usually, from four to six doors, to which roads led from every side; to guide wayfarers, a large candle burned on a pedestal all night . . . .

The Bruidhean Da Derga was burned by the foster-brothers of King Conaire Mor; Conaire was 87th in succession from Eremon Eber, and ascended the throne in 109 BC. His foster-brothers' lawless conduct caused him to banish them, whereupon they took to piracy, and, with a band of robbers, marched on Tara, pillaging and burning. Conaire was returning from Munster, and finding Meath devastated, turned by Dublin to Bohernabreena, where he was welcomed by his friend Da Derga; but the pirates hastened to the Bruidhean, slew the king on the hearthstone of his host, and burned the hostel.

The story in the Dinnseanchas sets the hostel on the River Dodder. King Conaire, after the hostel had been burned three times by the attackers, was thirsty. His cup-bearer valiantly forced a way through the enemy to the river but found that it had inconveniently run dry. So he embarked on a rapid circuit of Ireland in the course of which he found that all the other rivers were equally drought-stricken. By the time he returned Conaire had perished miserably.

There are other unlikely episodes in the tale, including the observation that the pirates while at sea had been able to make out the chariots parked around the hostel. All of which is acceptable in a myth. What is amazing is that as recently as 1935 an antiquarian named Henry Morris attempted in a learned paper to define the site of the hostel. With due contempt for the views of his predecessors he transferred the location of the story to a sort of hybrid between the headwaters of the Dodder (Mareen's Brook, derived, he argued, from the eclipsed *mbruidhin*) and those of the Glencree River. The pirates, he pointed out, had espied from the sea off the Wicklow coast candle-light shining through the chariot wheels. It was quite a candle, visible for twenty kilometres.

Other antiquarians located the action in other sites, Sir Samuel Ferguson favouring Donnybrook. Bohernabreena at least incorporates a hostel in its name without recourse to grammatical adjustment and its position just on the edge of the mountains seems logical enough. The certainty that the tale is not a meticulously accurate account of the engagement and the possibility that it never took place at all will probably discourage future scholars from the search for the hostel of Dá Derga.

Of much greater importance is the fact that this is an established otter place: spraints were found here in February 1990 and had been recorded also in a survey ten years earlier.

Fort Bridge

The graceful single arch of Fort Bridge was built in the 1830s. It is marred by strengthening iron joists on one side and a great black water main on the other. The 15-inch pipe, part of the conduit laid in 1884, carries the water from the upper lake of Glenasmole to the Ballyboden filtration plant 6 km distant and 76 metres lower down. The great waterfall has been shrouded in geometrical concrete and the water descends by three great steps. This desecration of a lovely rocky place is all that remains of a long-abandoned hydro-electric works.

The falls stand at the head of a deep gorge, so narrow that the sun seldom reaches the dark and mysterious pool below. The waterfall comes where a rock outcrop has prevented the river from cutting a gradual slope in the glacial till. On the right, immediately downstream of the bridge there is a large and splendid rock cliff, vertical and laminated on the upstream side, massive downstream. The laminated part is shale of Ordovician age, between 400 and 500 million years old. It is formed from a muddy sediment, deposited in a coastal lagoon. Intense pressure brought about the laminated structure and earth movements made the shale stand vertically.

The massive rock beside the shale is an intrusion of dolerite, which forced its way into the older rock in a molten state. This is an outlying 'sill' associated with the much bigger intrusion nearby which forms Ballymorefinn. There are rock outcrops on the left bank as well and then the edges of the gorge change from rock to grey clay with big blocks of limestone embedded in it. This material is typical of the glacial till derived from the limestone plain to the north.

Below Fort Bridge the Piperstown Stream joins the Dodder, nowadays a rather unhappy drain from the rubbish tip conveying water of doubtful purity. William Handcock tells of its earlier history:

Below this is Bohernabreena Bridge, built about forty years ago, across a very narrow part of the river, where formerly there was a plank thrown over it as a footbridge, at a spot called the Sheep-hole, which is a deep eddy under a steep rock. It is much used for washing sheep, and abounds with fine trout, which are fished for most assiduously all the season by Dubliners.

A stile crosses the fence on the left of the bridge giving access to a track which follows the river for about 1 km to the farm at Kiltipper House, through green cattle pasture. The steep, hazel-covered banks away to the left were carved out of the hillside by the Dodder before it cut down into the gorge. A similar abandoned bank runs close to the road on the far side. Between them the ground is nearly level. This level space is one of the terraces which mark a succession of periods when the river alternated between meandering to form a broad valley with a bed of gravel or silt and cutting its way downwards to form steep banks. The present deep gorge has been cut more recently and, unless prevented by man, will ultimately become wider and wider and form a similar terrace at a lower level.

The river bank is dangerous and cattle and people are kept at a safe distance from it by a barbed wire fence on the left side and by a much more impenetrable chain-link on the right. So there are only glimpses of the river as it winds its way through the gorge. About 100 metres downstream of the bridge the river runs between great bastions of slate. Then the valley widens and there are gravel banks below Kiltipper House. An alternative name for the spot was Diana. The scene of meandering river with beds of gravel on either side and steep banks some way back is the present day equivalent of the appearance of the stretch just below Fort Bridge before the gorge was cut.

Kiltipper and the highest mills

On the left bank there is a little collection of ruined stone buildings, almost obliterated but with a curious circular structure remaining. About 3 metres in diameter and one metre high, it is neatly built and now almost overgrown by a remnant of a hawthorn tree and an effusion of blackberry.

These probably are the last mortal remains of the highest mill in the valley, marked on the 1838 map as a 'parchment mill' and powered by the Ballinascorney Stream before it was diverted to the upper lake. Downstream lies the neat farm of Kiltipper and below that the pasture on the left bank has been replaced by scrub, with gorse the dominant plant.

Across the river there is well-fenced pasture thinly scattered with bungalows. Up above them the rose window of Bohernabreena Church looks out over the valley. It was built in 1870 on an ancient religious site and replaced a church of penal days. This seems to me to be the ideal site for Dá Derga's Hostel and no less a scholar than O'Curry might agree. It has a commanding position at the entrance to the enchanted gorge of Glenasmole and a lovely view of Dublin Bay.

Down in the valley there was a weir, the highest on the Dodder in the old days. It has disappeared and that is scarcely surprising. Mallet the engineer wrote with professional disdain of its state in 1844: 'an ill-constructed weir of loose stones and sods'. From the weir a millrace flowed northwards for nearly 1 km to Oldbawn paper mill which

A landslip caused by undercutting of the cliff at Oldbawn.

stood close to the site of the modern church and community centre. William Handcock visited the mill some time before 1876 when business was thriving and I quote from his detailed and enthusiastic description of the state-of-the-art works which he saw:

> The mill is now the property of a company, of which Mr. M'Donnell is the manager. Several of the Dublin journals are supplied from it. The paper is principally made of Esparto grass and straw, with some admixture of rags . . . . The machinery is driven by a steam-engine of 200 horse power, and by several smaller ones, besides a large waterwheel, forty feet in diameter.

But this must have been near the end of its days. The 1899 edition of Handcock's book has the disheartening footnote:

> The mill has been closed since the above was written. The company were unable to compete with foreign manufacture. The place is now a desert.

The millrace supplied a large pond near Oldbawn House and then flowed on to power, in Mallet's time, McCracken's flour mill, also known as Haarlem, about 600 metres north of Oldbawn Bridge. In 1776 the mill was run by Haarlem and Co., calico printers and, as in the case of the other cloth printing works, had a great bleach green nearby. In 1813 a Mr Bewley was one of the owners and perhaps the first of the Quaker family to live and work in the Dodder valley.

The Haarlem Mill has been replaced by a housing estate which pays tribute to the memory in its name of Millbrook Lawns. There were three more mills just downstream: one flour and two woollen. One more, Williamson's pasteboard mill, lay 800m farther on. Then the tailrace rejoined its parent Dodder a little way upstream of Firhouse. At the time when all these mills were in operation, and Kiltipper weir in good repair, hardly any water flowed in the main channel.

The level of water pollution was a great deal worse than anything now known in Ireland. The chemical residues of paper and pasteboard mills are likely to have killed all the fish and insects that should have been there. They did more than that, to quote Handcock once more:

> . . . the river here joins the city water-course. The citizens are fortunate that they are not now dependent on it, for it is so polluted by the paper-making that it has become poisonous, and cattle and horses have died from drinking it. Sometimes it is the same colour as porter.

The passing of water mills is always a tragedy — but the demise of the effluents makes it easier to bear.

Handcock seems to have walked all the way down the Dodder within the parish of Tallaght and to have taken careful notes as he went. His record, made more than a century ago, describes the state of the river long before heavy machinery was used to bring it under control or to quarry the gravel — and before the waterworks at Glenasmole made some contribution to stemming the floods. Men with shovels did the digging, horses and carts removed the stone:

> The rapid floods, caused by the steepness of the sides of the catchment basin, carry down great quantities of mud and shingle. The latter is now mostly deposited above the city weir at Firhouse, forming an inexhaustible supply of rather bad road material. Probably not less than 4,000 tons are, and have been for many years, annually removed. The consequence is, that the bed of the river below Kiltipper has been lowered several feet, the river now running in a deep channel, in some places reaching to the rock, but principally cut in the blue clay . . .
>
> Many have been the attempts, and large the sums of money spent by various riparian proprietors in striving to reclaim portions of the extensive strands between Kiltipper and Fir-House. Costly walls have been built, and as often undermined and levelled by this turbulent river; bridges have been swept away and new tracts of ground devastated. Of late years, owing to the channel having become so deep, the river has become more tractable, and has not done so much damage.

Rocks and soils of Oldbawn

On the right bank access to the river across the pasture is difficult and the owners have festooned their gates with barbed wire to keep it that way. A pitch and putt course stands at the bottom of a remarkable ridged hill which has, as long as I can remember, always been bright green with grass rather than covered in hazel scrub like most of the hillsides nearby. The geological map marks it as gravel deposited by a torrent of melt water from the ice.

The road from Bohernabreena Church joins the riverside road at the north end of the pitch and putt. It doesn't have the look of a highway of note but there have been suggestions that it follows the path of the legendary Slighe Cualann, one of the five great routes leading from Tara to the uttermost parts of the kingdom. The junction is also said to mark the spot where a great geological fault crosses the Dodder running from east to west. The geologists are probably on more solid ground (as geologists tend to be) than the medievalists. But the blanket of glacial till is so thick that the exact position of the fault is a matter for conjecture.

Nevertheless it certainly exists and, even though the upheavals took place three hundred million years ago, the fault has had a profound influence on the history of humankind in the Dodder valley. The fault line runs from Blackrock across the Dodder and onwards for about 1 kilometre where it is crossed by a north-south fault from Clondalkin to Glenasmole. Along the east-west fault the ancient Ordovician slates and the granite were thrust upwards breaking through the overlying limestone. The limestone at its new higher level was eroded more quickly than that which stayed lower down. So the older rocks were revealed and, what is more important than their age, they had no lime. Acid rocks in the highlands form barren moorland while limestone means fertility and ultimately rich agricultural land. So the invaders settled near Dublin and left the regions south of Oldbawn and the fault to the dispossessed.

A tannery spreads over a large area between road and river opposite the pitch and putt and a good deal of dumping of rubble has taken place across the river from it.

Considerable areas of dilapidation confront the wayfarer who can only hope that the County Council will take it all in hand some day. The most interesting feature is the iron water main which carries Liffey water from Saggart to Ballyboden where it meets the supply from the Dodder. Both can make their way thence to Stillorgan to join with the other great 19th-century aqueduct from the Vartry.

Oldbawn bridges and ghosts

Downstream from the water main the river is crossed by the graceful arch of Oldbawn Bridge, of limestone with granite borders and a granite string course. Built into the downstream wall at both sides are 'pyramidal abutments', tapering pillars of limestone blocks, rough-hewn on the outside. Some small stalactites hang from the mortar on the arch. It spans a high waterfall, built of limestone blocks but repaired at the edges with concrete.

Handcock had been unduly pessimistic about the bridge:

> . . . a fine arch of one span, built about 1840. There was a bridge of three arches on the same spot before: but it only

Granite sills on the sluice control at Firhouse.

stood for about forty years, when, becoming undermined, it had to be taken down. The present one is not likely to last as long. Unless some care is taken, down it must come. Below this the bed of the river becomes very wide, and there are acres of shingle and waste land extending to the City Weir at Fir-House.

Evidently some care was taken and there are signs of much engineering work since his day. The water descends by four great steps. Below the fall, the river flows at the bottom of a gorge, the left bank protected by enormous boulders of dolerite from Ballinascorney quarry, the right nearly vertical, a cliff of grey glacial till.

On the left bank, upstream of the bridge, is Oldbawn House, a pleasant 19th-century farmhouse surrounded by outbuildings which have happily survived immersion in a housing estate. It stands on the site of the 17th-century mansion of the same name built by Archdeacon William Bulkely. A splendid sculptured chimney piece from that house, bearing the date 1635, is preserved in the National Museum. There are grim records of the devastation of Oldbawn by the Cromwellians in 1641, but more settled times followed, the family fortunes were restored and Bulkely died in comfort there in 1671. If you are unlucky you will see the phantom coach of the archdeacon, drawn by six headless horses. He (or in these enlightened days, she) whose path it crosses dies within a year and a day. Consequently there are very few people around who have enjoyed the privilege of viewing the apparition.

The linear park

Downstream of the bridge the County Council has turned the level space of the river terrace into playing fields. The steep banks have been smoothed to form a gently curving slope down towards the river. The park was opened in 1987. A footpath runs close to the river's edge, bordered by poplars, willows, birch and alders amongst other trees. The poplars are exotics and the aim of the park authorities is to use native trees as far as possible. A problem lies in the fact that the natives grow rather slowly and it takes a long time before they are big enough to be safe from vandalism. The poplars grow faster and recover more quickly if they get broken. So they act as nurses to the more delicate trees and can be thinned when these are well grown and strong enough to stand up for themselves. Maybe by that time the first generation of vandals will be grown up too and their successors may take a more enlightened view of the environment.

The land on the right bank was largely in private hands and often inhabited by a herd of cattle. To further the development of the park by the riverside, the County Council served Compulsory Acquisition Orders on the landowners. In the celebrated Shortt Case in the High Court in 1983 compensation of £84,000 per acre was awarded. So high was the rate that the Orders on the neighbouring land were revoked. As a result, instead of the prospect of a wide open space, shops and housing are encroaching between road and river. The positive achievement has been an agreement to preserve public access to the riverside and a footpath will be provided. It will therefore continue to be possible to walk along either bank.

Both sides of the valley from Oldbawn downstream are incorporated in the Dodder Valley Linear Park which is planned ultimately to cover 300 acres (122 hectares) within the County Council's jurisdiction. This extends as far as Bushy Park and 200 acres are already in public ownership.

Until the end of 1989, the land at the top of the cliff above the right bank was faintly wildernessy — inasmuch as cattle pasture ever merits this description. Shopping centres and houses then grew with astonishing rapidity, but old stone walls and hedges, often overgrown with blackberry, remain and make a habitat for robins, wrens and hedge sparrows. The planting of more hawthorns and other shrubs in due course will add to the attractions.

Changing landforms

The river curves towards the right for 150 metres and as a result its margin on that side is a nearly vertical cliff, from time to time getting undercut and falling away, so maintaining its steepness. A landslip in March 1989 left a pile of clay lumps with, about half way up the cliff, a band of grass which had fallen from the top. The loosened clay

The restored sluice gate at Firhouse.

gradually gets carried away and the cliff returns to its vertical profile, but a little farther to the right than before.

Water in a river moves faster on the outside of a curve
and therefore has more power for eroding it. On the inner
side the current is slower and the eroded material is
dumped so that a bank builds up. This is disguised by the
landscaping at Old Bawn but may be seen clearly at the
next left-hand curve. A gravel bank lies inside the curve
and protects the cliff from rushing water. At this point,
and similar ones lower down, material which falls from the
cliff stays near its base and the slope becomes steep rather
than vertical. Grasses, gorse, blackberry, wild rose and
many other species of flowering plants are able to gain a
foothold and ultimately the glacial till gets completely
hidden.

Where the river swings right again the cliff appears once
more. The glacial till is grey, a fine-grained muddy matrix,
with frequent large lumps of limestone. In *The Geology of
Dublin* H. J. Seymour describes the remarkable variety of
rock types to be found in the banks of the Dodder:

> In character this limestone-drift of the Dodder bluffs is a
> stiff blue-gray highly calcareous till, full of scratched lime-
> stone blocks and pebbles, with occasional fragments of
> Silurian grit, Old Red Sandstone conglomerate, basic
> igneous rocks, including some of the Lambay porphyry
> type, hard chalk like that of County Antrim, and occasion-
> ally granites of the north.
>
> . . . Part of the boulder clay in this district is of a brown
> colour, and contains shell fragments . . . and rather numer-
> ous far-travelled pebbles. This is well seen in the river-
> section west of Rathfarnham, and again north-west of
> Butterfield House, where the brown clay overlies the dark
> blue-gray limestone-clay of the usual type.

The shells identified included cockles (though not mussels)
and 14 other species of shellfish which are common in the
shallow parts of the sea today. The ice which carried the
material therefore had filled the basin of the Irish Sea. As
for the rock fragments, the fact that granite from the
Mountains of Mourne and chalk from County Antrim
have been carried for such distances makes a fair bid to

equal the fantasies of the tales of the Fianna.

About 500 metres downstream from the bridge, a deposit of coarse gravel lies on top of the till on the right bank, a trace of another of the river terraces. The gravel resembles that of the present day river bed down beneath it and was deposited by the river, perhaps thousands of years ago, when it flowed at a higher level. Gravel deposits of this kind have been quarried away over much of the area. This particular one may have been too small to be considered worthwhile. Downstream of this point, a layer of the brown sea-bed material, about 50 cm thick, lies on top of the main mass of blue-grey till.

At the next strong left-hand swing the County Council has taken the right bank in hand, placing a long line of stones and rubble close to the water's edge to prevent further erosion. This leaves a very interesting stretch of gravelly soil where many wild flowers grow. Downstream there are large beds of watercress. This is the true edible kind, distinguished by its round rather than pointed leaves. Then the river widens and begins to branch to form a number of islands. Even though the cress itself may be good to eat, there is an element of sewage pollution in the river and therefore no knowing what might coat the leaves.

The sand martin colony

On the right, a colony of sand martins has excavated about 30 tunnels in a deposit of firm grey sandy material 2 metres above the level of the water.

Sand martin

Arriving in March or April after an unhurried journey from south of the Equator, the sand martins stay around until October when they go south once more, unable to survive the shortage of small flying insects in the Irish winter. Amongst the most delightful birds of the Dodder valley, they are confined to a feeding area within a few miles of the nesting colony. They excavate tunnels about one metre long, sloping slightly uphill into the bank. The composition of the bank must be exactly right for them: if it is too hard they are unable to burrow, but at the same time it must be firm enough not to collapse.

All through the summer the sand martins come and go. Activity increases when the young hatch and have to be fed on hundreds of small insects daily. In the early stages the parents scuffle to the end of the tunnel each time they come to feed the helpless brood in the nest chamber at the end. When they have grown a little, the chicks walk to the opening and poke their heads out, waiting for the parents to arrive with the next meal.

Provided the weather stays reasonably fine, they lead secure lives: cats and rats are unable to climb the river bank and no predatory birds are able to enter the tunnels. The only serious risk is of a long spell of rainy weather preventing the flight of the prey insects. Because of the scarcity of exactly the right type of mud bank, sand martin colonies are few and far between and this one deserves special protection, particularly as it can be seen and enjoyed by so many people.

Above the sand martin colony the cliff is high and at the top there is a deep layer of the brown material. On the right a bank with hawthorn bushes shows a former meander of the river at a higher level and there is a similar high bank on the left. But the geography is not quite as easy as it seems. Sticking out from near the clifftop, but firmly embedded in the brown soil are two slabs of cement. They were certainly not buried by the primeval river nor transported by the Midlandian ice. Evidently the bank here has been pushed about by a bulldozer — though a relatively long time ago, long enough for a grass sward to be well established on top of it all.

Herons nest in a group of trees some way back from the river bank here. Heron or, to be very precise, 'grey heron' is the correct name of those gangling, long-legged birds with enormous wings. They are often called 'crane' but real crane birds are very much bigger and are now extremely rare in Ireland and indeed over most of western Europe. Before roads were built and swamps drained they were plentiful. The heron has survived and has adapted remarkably well to suburban life where the Dodder flows. Herons are never really plentiful: they need a large extent of river to provide enough food. They feed mainly on small fish but the fish by and large are hard for the heron to see so that it spends most of the time watching and waiting.

The island wilderness

If you close your eyes to the occasional corpses of supermarket trollies and cars, the gravel banks provide small oases of true wilderness in the suburbs, interesting, like the vertical cliffs, in owing practically nothing to the human hand. Nearly all our familiar countryside landscapes are man-made. Only cliffs and water-borne sand and gravel make a bid to be considered as truly natural. Thanks to the Dodder's propensity for violent flooding, debris, often including trees and bushes, gets swept downstream and the river bed is replaced partly by newly exposed gravel, partly by material carried from upstream and dumped.

When the floods abate, new banks and islets appear, waiting to be colonised by a specialised community of wild flowers. Because the more stable, dry land habitats are either heavily grazed or frequently mown or tilled, the variety of wild flowers is limited. But nobody tries to do anything with the ground between the banks of the river and the flowers are left to themselves. What is more, because of the flooding, the bushes or trees which would suppress many of the flowers cannot establish themselves.

One hundred and seventy-nine different species of flowering plant have been recorded from the region around the Dodder between Old Bawn and Firhouse — the survey included hedges and pasture, but a great many of the flowers came from the riverside itself. With the help of the botanist, Sylvia Reynolds, I made a list of more than 60 species between the banks of the river on an afternoon early in September — and that was only a casual visit lasting less than an hour.

Some of them were particularly interesting or beautiful or both. The monkey flower has spread all the way down here from its point of origin in Glenasmole. Fat hen, a rather unprepossessing dark green herb, is plentiful. The seeds were used for poultry fodder — hence the name —

but in Viking Dublin there is evidence that people used them to make porridge for their own consumption. Dyer's rocket, another biggish herb with yellow-green flowers, was first recorded in Dublin as long ago as 1727 when Caleb Threlkeld wrote 'It is sown for Dyers, and grows spontaneously upon Rubbish and Fallow fields . . . .' A yellow dye used to be made from it.

Sally

Plants such as coltsfoot and silver weed are truly native species which colonise dry stony places in all parts of the country. Others, including the monkey flower, are recent arrivals. Among the aliens is one of the most abundant of the riverside flowers, the winter heliotrope, which has big almost circular leaves and produces pale purple flowers in midwinter. It is a native of Italy and was introduced in the middle of the 19th century to provide winter feeding for bees if they happened to be tempted outside on warm days. Probably the most recent arrival is a mustard plant with tall, stringy almost leafless stems and clumps of about ten small yellow flowers. It arrived in Dublin port a few years ago, established itself at Ringsend and proceeded to migrate around the city and up the Dodder.

The islands are largely overgrown with willow and alder. Willows are more plentiful on the level ground, alder on the banks. There are at least three different willow species there, sometimes all of them growing together in small groups. Crack willow has long leaves, dark on the underside. The twigs snap off easily at the joints which explains the name. The other two are sally, with rather broad, oval leaves which have rusty brown hairs on the lower side, and osier with narrow leaves, nearly white underneath. In the days of basket-making it was the most important species. Many generations of willows live on the islands, including dozens of young ones which have sprung up from seed or by the rooting of twigs broken off in the floods and carried downstream.

Birds and frogs and dragonflies

Long-tailed tit

The thicket formed by the willows and alders is rich in bird life. Obviously the willow warbler is to be expected. Except when singing on a conspicuous perch — which the males do ceaselessly from spring to early summer — the willow warblers keep fairly well hidden. Delicate colouring of olive green and pale yellow makes them almost invisible amongst the leaves. Parties of long-tailed tits can nearly always be seen: tiny birds with tails longer than their bodies which hunt busily for insects amongst the branches. The rather uncommon siskin, a bright yellow-green finch, is a frequent visitor in winter, often in the company of redpolls, small brown finches with little crimson patches on the head. These seldom stay in one place for long, but move up and down the river, concentrating on the willows and alder. Meadow pipits can usually be seen at this point, often perching on the overhead wires. Needing open spaces, their range does not extend much farther down the river.

Large, almost stagnant, ponds have been formed amongst the islands. These add to the variety of water plants and allow frogs and newts and some of the most spectacular insects to live hereabout. Frogs and newts both need undisturbed water to spawn in — their tadpoles cannot survive in running water, nor can they live in lakes because trout and perch like to eat them. Newts spend their lives in the ponds, but frogs leave the water as soon as they are big enough and hunt for insects in the grass. In winter they return to the water, burrow into the mud and sleep through the cold weather. They emerge in February to enjoy mating games in the water, lay their eggs and return to the damp grasses again.

Neither frogs nor newts are as plentiful as they used to be. Land drainage in particular has greatly reduced their habitat. They are therefore accorded special protection in wildlife legislation all over Europe. The collection and possession of frog spawn is forbidden by law — but you can easily get a permit to keep it from the Wildlife Service Headquarters in Leeson Lane.

Dragonflies are insects which need the comfort and safety of quiet pools with muddy beds. The larvae of the bigger kinds burrow into the mud when resting, leaving the burrows to stalk and capture smaller insects. They are able to swim by jet propulsion if they need to go somewhere in a hurry. The larvae take one or two years to become fully grown and ready to leave the water. The adults emerge in summer and take to the air. The sympetrum is one of the common species on the Dodder: females have yellow bodies, males bright red and both have enormous eyes. They like to rest on stones in the sun in the intervals between darting around hunting for flies. In wet or cold weather the dragonflies, and butterflies too, keep out of sight and avoid flying but they seem to appear from nowhere when the sun comes to stay.

Cowslip

Gravel and concrete

On the left bank at the bottom of a rubbish-strewn cliff there lies another ox-bow lake. Thrilling though it be to geomorphologists, this place of black mud and stagnant water is not the most aesthetically pleasing point of the Dodder. However, even this is worth preserving. A number of water plants live there which are scarce elsewhere on the river and the future development of this mud-patch will be extremely interesting. If left undisturbed, the pool will gradually fill up and a succession of different plants will live there as the ground grows drier. This will take many years and provide generations of school classes with an example of a developing landform.

Pylons carry high tension wires across the river above the islands. Beneath them on the right bank a large, unlikely and unprepossessing expanse of concrete covers the ground. It is all that remains of a block factory which existed as long as suitable gravel could be won from the surroundings and has been derelict for many years. Rubbish and cars have been dumped there and along the edge there are spoil heaps which may once have protected the factory from high floods. Winter heliotrope covers these mounds almost completely and provides a touch of pale colour in December and January. Many lime-loving plants, including yellow wort and bird's foot trefoil, grow there.

The demise of the gravel pits, which were especially plentiful near Firhouse, was hastened by the damming of the Dodder in Glenasmole. In the days of its freedom the river in flood transported enormous quantities of clay and gravel, scoured out of the banks of glacial till. The clay is carried in suspension as microscopic particles, much of it all the way to the sea. The gravel moves for much smaller distances since the stones and large sand grains get dropped as soon as the speed of the current is reduced to normal levels.

In the old days the gravel excavated in or around Firhouse was continually being replaced by more from the mountains. The dams and weirs of the waterworks prevented this free flow and the mountain gravel is all deposited in Glenasmole. The erosion of the valley is also being reduced by the great boulders which the County Council are placing on the edges of the river. These, like the weirs, reduce the speed of the water and likewise its power of tearing away the banks.

In spite of the presence there of interesting wild flowers, it can reasonably be argued that the appearance of the area of concrete slabs could be improved. Unlike so much of the land beside the river, there is nothing on the concrete that conservationists wish to conserve and the planners of the linear park have an opportunity to change the site for the better. Should it come into public ownership, there is a very exciting scheme to transform this part of the valley into a 'major water feature', preserving the islands and their thicket but creating in addition a lake which can be expected to attract a variety of water birds. Black-headed gulls have nested there now and again.

Going downstream, there is cattle pasture on the right, fenced by a trace of an old hedge with hawthorn and elder and a remnant of a stone wall. Early in summer, the pasture is bright with the delicate flowers of cowslip, a very familiar plant in the lime-rich lowlands of County Dublin but singled out for special protection in Great Britain on account of its rarity there.

The high stone wall belongs to the convent of the Carmelite Sisters who moved there in 1827 from Clondalkin, to a house said to be over four hundred years old. They ran a school until 1851 which they then handed over to the Board of Education. The school grew over the years: two teachers in 1868, four in 1954 and a new school built on land which the Sisters donated and now grown to need 16 teachers.

Between the Convent fields and the river there is a level patch where gorse and other shrubs are growing. Grass in Ireland thrives only where it is eaten or mown. As soon as grazing is prevented, as in this case by a boundary fence, gorse and thorn trees establish themselves. In the course of time trees will grow up from seed. Oak, ash, wild cherry and holly represent the native vegetation but, ever since its introduction in the 17th century, sycamore has often dominated. Its wind-borne seeds are very viable and the tree itself can somehow survive in the most unlikely situations: on walls or on cliffs.

Just what to do with a piece of waste ground like this is a difficult problem. Left to itself it will form an impenetrable jungle for a long, long time: fifty years or even more. Ultimately, the trees will grow, shade out the shrubs and produce a forest which can live for centuries. While the individual trees seldom survive for more than a couple of hundred years, they don't all die at the same time and those that fall get replaced first by scrub and ultimately by a new tree.

But to leave the scrub with the grazing animals fenced out is as artificial as laying down a lawn or raising a crop of hay. Not one of the possible treatments can claim to be more 'natural' than another. The gorse scrub, as it develops, is a good habitat for many small birds. There are rabbits there and probably foxes. To leave it on its own, except for maintaining a footpath or two, might be the most acceptable treatment. There is plenty of lawn and pasture nearby and the development of the scrub will be very interesting to watch.

Firhouse Weir and the City Watercourse

Downstream of this patch comes one of the highlights of the Dodder valley, the great weir of Firhouse: not just a truly splendid artificial waterfall but an integral part of a waterworks established more than seven hundred years ago.

The weir itself was rebuilt after the floods of Hurricane Charlie damaged it severely. The construction is mainly of very large blocks of limestone and the water descends in two great steps, passing over a level concrete sill. Above the weir the river forms a lovely deep, calm pool where moorhens swim or stride along the crest of the weir, displaying their long, pale green legs. In summer their totally delightful chicks appear, little black downy things like animated golf balls, busily scurrying about on the surface or pattering on the shore. Sometimes a kingfisher perches on a branch above the water.

On the right bank there is one pair of sluice gates, controlling the level and allowing water to overflow down a chute between limestone masonry walls. The coping and sill of the sluice are of granite and the gates are controlled by turning enormous brass nuts. On the left the sluice

Lattice girder bridge

arrangement is much more complicated. A stream runs off towards the east: this is the City Watercourse, excavated before 1244 to carry water to the River Poddle and so to St James's Gate. To me that little bit of watercourse is more than history: it is also a deep pool with long-established mud which is an ideal haunt for young dragonflies, for minnows and for many fascinating water insects.

One set of sluices controls the current in the Watercourse and another allows for an overflow, returning the water to the Dodder down below. At the foot of the weir the water runs gently over a gravelly bed, almost hidden in summer by a green carpet of water cress. Up above this you may cross the ravine by an ancient bridge, built in 1861. I had always loved it anyway and enjoyed looking down at the sparkling river over the edges or even through the gaps in the old timbers. But it took the artist's eye of Maurice Craig to reveal to me that it is 'a lattice girder bridge with an elegant subtle camber' and I had to go and examine it once more. It is slightly hidden by sycamores and bushes but you can appreciate the gentle curve from the riverside under the weir.

Handcock describes how the place looked in the 1840s when the City Watercourse took the entire flow of the river except in floods:

> Thirty years ago it was easy to drive across below the weir: in fact, it was the main road to Tallaght and the Greenhills. Now there is a precipitous bank of twenty feet deep on each side, and it is impassable. For many years the only way of crossing from Fir-House during a flood was by the dangerous one of wading along the top of the weir. The water rushes with great force, although of little depth; and if the foot slipped the consequences might be fatal.
>
> Long ago there was a wooden foot-bridge put up below the weir by subscription; but this was soon swept away in a flood, and the planks floated down to Ringsend. About fifteen years ago, a neat iron lattice-bridge was put up for foot-passengers, which is still in good order. It is twenty feet above the bed of the river, and about the level of the old road. Below the weir, the river receives two streams from Mont Pelier; and passing in front of the paper-mills, where there was another ford, it spread over a wide bed of shingle

opposite Spawell. This was reclaimed by Mr Fowler of Cherryfield, and the river runs in a straight, deep course to Kilvare.

The rape of the Dodder

On the 29th April, 1244, Maurice Fitzgerald, Justiciar of Ireland, issued a writ commanding the Sheriff of Dublin, without delay, with the advice of the Mayor and citizens, to make inquisition by twelve free men, as jurors, as to the place from which water could be best and most conveniently taken from its course, and conducted to the King's city of Dublin, for the benefit of the city, and at the cost of the citizens.

While 1244 is thus the first definite date for the works at Firhouse Weir, Val Jackson who published a paper on the subject in 1951 wrote:

> There can be no doubt that the Dodder works at Balrothery were the property of the Abbey of St Thomas for a considerable period before the Dodder water supply was laid on to the city and that these works continued to be the property of the Abbey until at least 1259. It is also clear that the Mandate of 1244 did not initiate these works but referred solely to the watercourse

and added:

> There is good reason for believing that the boundary course was completed and that the Dodder water had reached the Barony of St. Thomas not later than the end of 1243 (OS).

The purpose of the weir at this point on the Dodder was to divert water to the Poddle, about 2 km distant. The Poddle, rising near Tallaght, enters the Liffey close to the old city of Dublin while the Dodder actually flows away from the city to the east. The Watercourse continued to supply the millers and other citizens throughout the centuries and it is frequently mentioned in the annals.

In 1685 Sir William Petty, describing the Barony of Newcastle and Uppercrosse, wrote:

... the South east part of the Barony is watered by the River Dogher which is a river that Descends by many branches from the Mountaines which being United, doth after greate raines overflow soe yt many tymes both man and beasts are cast away by the Violence of the sudden flood but havinge the Sea to empty itself into is in a very lytle time abated. One maine branch of this river is separated by Artificial helps, at the Townelande of Templeoge to Convey water to the Citty . . . .

... the Residue of the said River at Templeogue passes to Rafarnam and there Meeteth with another branch: passinge into the Channell on the South West of Ringsend on this branch had stood many Corn and Tuck Mills which have been harmed by the late War but some of them have beene lately repaired . . . .

The Dodder and Poddle provided the main supply of water to the city until the Liffey was tapped at Islandbridge in 1735 and the Canals in 1773. The Dodder, however, continued to be essential in the supply of water power to nine mills on the Watercourse. By the middle of the 19th century the weir was in a thoroughly dilapidated state and Robert Mallet wrote in 1844:

The whole weir is in a ruinous condition; the apron is wholly gone; the bed of the river 4 to 6 feet below the toe of the pitching, which is deeply undermined; the discharging sluice decayed, and constantly staunched with turf mould and litter; and the whole structure in danger of being carried away by some heavy flood . . . .

You can only speculate now as to whether any part of the present day weir goes back to the 13th century. But there is an air of great antiquity in the exceptionally large size of the limestone blocks used. Generally speaking, considerably smaller stones were used in works of this kind in the 18th and 19th centuries. What the medieval engineers did achieve was the construction of a weir of the height of the present day structure — anything lower could not have supplied the head of water required to join up with the River Poddle. Although the crest height above sea level must have been about the same as nowadays, the actual height of the weir could have been less. The Dodder downstream of the weir in the 13th century may have been flowing at the level of the lawn on the right bank.

The sluices on the left bank do not stand in their original positions. They had to be moved and rebuilt to make room for the road. Its construction, together with a functional concrete bridge in 1987, have made dramatic changes in the appearance of the valley. Happily, the girder bridge is still in place, if badly needing a coat of paint and replacement of the woodwork; the weir has received tender loving care and there are plans for cleaning up the surroundings.

Downstream of Bella Vista, the house on the left bank on the north side of the new road, a little bit of clambering over hedges and ditches gives access first to the Water-course — in dry weather mainly course with very little water — and then to the river bank. The meadows, mown for hay in June each year, are the property of the County Council which has exciting plans to let the stream flow again and to develop a water garden. Hawthorn is the dominant bush along the watercourse which runs beneath Scots pines in the Bella Vista grounds and sycamores elsewhere.

Firhouse weir.

The remains of a tarmac path run along the river bank between the wall of the ancient farmyard of Spawell House and the river which flows at the bottom of steep cliffs of glacial till. It is grey material, much coarser than the deposits between Old Bawn and Firhouse, made up mainly of limestone with relatively little clay. Opposite Spawell it contains a yellow-brown layer of finer material, perhaps a deposit of silt from an earlier and higher Dodder. There once were gravel pits above this, but they have been worked out and abandoned. The right bank downstream is being undercut and an old wall is now teetering on the edge, ready to fall down and be carried away before very long. The bed of the river is crossed by a series of low weirs of stone built by the anglers to create pools for trout.

Spawell and Cherryfield

Spawell was praised by Weston Joyce in 1912 as the 'once famous spa of Templeogue, where the wealth, the beauty and the fashion of Dublin were wont to assemble one hundred and eighty years ago'. Dr Rutty, the naturalist employed by the Dublin Society (now the RDS) wrote that the water lost its medicinal properties between the years 1749 and 1751. Fortunately the house survived and remains in good order to this day. Built between 1712 and 1730, it predates the general run of classical Irish houses. The windows of the third storey stand between the slopes of the high-pitched roof. The outbuildings are equally ancient and, with the house, are listed for preservation.

The land on the right bank between road and river from Firhouse Bridge to the sharp bend of the Dodder at Knocklyon Road is nearly all the property of the County Council which is working steadily to preserve it as a park. Broad green fields extend for nearly a mile, divided by old stone walls and hedges with many fine old trees. Much of the ground is level. Five playing fields exist there at present and there are plans for tennis courts and a car park. The old house of Cherryfield was so severely damaged by vandals that it had to be demolished early in 1987. The site, phoenix-like, is to be used for new buildings for dressing rooms for athletes and an interpretation centre for contemplatives.

From the bridge at Firhouse you can walk, with a little climbing of hedges, down the right bank through a slightly unkempt unfenced field between river and road. The Dodder runs between steep, high banks except for a sort of ledge half-way down which has a dense shrubbery of snowberry. There is a healthy growth of hedge and scrub which often keeps the path a little way back from the river. But the natural barrier is broken in places so that you can take an occasional look at the water. Kingfishers like this stretch, as do herons and dippers.

Across the river, to the right of the pines and surrounded by show-jumping fences and the like, stands a strange tall building, of rough-cast on the lower storey and yellow brick above. It was the engine house of Francis Burke's flour mill which in former days had been the first of the nine mills on the City Watercourse.

On the right bank, one tiny cottage, still inhabited, stands where it was built more than one hundred and fifty years ago. It is marked on the 1837 map but much farther away from the riverside than nowadays. At the time of the first survey the Dodder ran straight past the house, 50 metres away from it. Since then the river has departed from its straight course and is gradually curving towards the cottage, which now has only 30 metres left. By the river bank an old field boundary wall is, bit by bit, breaking up and falling down the cliff.

Where the land is free from playing fields, the grass is cropped for hay. This is a very important undertaking from the point of view of encouraging wild flowers: many species are able to live amongst the grasses and produce their flowers before the hay is mown. The hedges consist mainly of hawthorn. One day, in September 1989, I counted the various bushes. Two thirds of them were hawthorn, 51 in all. Next were 8 blackthorn, 7 elder and 6 ash. There were just 2 wild roses and 1 sycamore. A row of Scots pines and a grove of poplars had been planted: the pines a long time ago, certainly fifty and maybe a hundred years. Because they were tall and their canopies allowed plenty of light to reach the ground, the hawthorns were able to form an understorey beneath them.

Hawthorn and blackthorn

Hawthorn is a native shrub and a very interesting one, too. There are many folk traditions, Irish and English, associated with it. Many a hawthorn tree has been preserved because of being under the special care of fairies and, in spite of my suburban background, I was brought up in the knowledge that I must never bring hawthorn flowers into the house. My mother as a child suffered from a misinterpretation of the English jingle:

> Ne'r cast a clout
> Till May be out.

Grannie held firmly that this meant the keeping on of winter woollies until the beginning of June. In fact may is another name for hawthorn which comes 'out' in April in a mild year.

Well grown, leafy hawthorns provide some of the best shelter for nesting song birds: blackbird, song thrush, chaffinch, greenfinch and hedge sparrow. The foliage keeps the nests well hidden and the thorny branches make an effective screen against cats and magpies. And finally, in autumn, the red berries provide abundant food for the thrushes. Hawthorn, thriving as it does on the limestone soil, is arguably the best of all bushes for planting in the parks of Dublin — to say nothing of being the most beautiful. Blackthorn makes sticks and grows sloes, the purple bitter berries which can be soaked in gin to make a drink like nectar.

The first bridge at Templeogue was built about 1800. Before that time, all vehicles going to or coming from the neighbourhood of Firhouse had to ford the river about a quarter of a mile upstream. The Dodder was much wider then, before its bed was restricted by the Drainage Commissioners of 1846. The name of the townland is derived from *Teach Mealóg* which was the form used in 14th-century documents. This presumably translates as the House of Mealóg — but history has little to say as to the identity of a householder of that name, except for the mention of a shadowy saint in the annals.

Austin Clarke

A new bridge, gently curved with a central span for the
river and smaller spans for people on both banks, replaces
the old stone arch. It had become too narrow for commut-
ing traffic undreamed of by the engineers of the end of the
18th century. The new one was named in honour of the
poet Austin Clarke who had lived nearby and deeply loved
the river:

> **On a bright morning**
> A blackbird sat on a sun-spot
> Warming his wings. Down by the bridge,
> Flying from our elm, fat pigeon
> > Had slowly got
> > Himself into hot
> Water. Along the garden walk
> The scattered crumbs still lay.
> Up in a pine, magpie was talking
> Too much. I whistled in vain, for the sparrows,
> After a dust-bath under the rose-buds,
> Had gone on a holiday
> To the river bend. I saw them play
> > A game of 'Shall we?'
> > 'Yes, Let's', beside the shallows
> Then feather the drops to spray.

Below the bridge a weir descends in four great steps of
limestone, the highest faced with granite. Slightly inaccessible because of the proximity and formidable fencing of
private gardens, it was built to control the floods which
were threatening to undermine the old bridge. Dippers
have nested in the weir, and maybe still do: I used to watch
them flying in through the curtain of water to a hidden site,
totally secure from predators. Grey wagtail and mallard
families enjoy the pool and the splashing water down
below. Herons nest in the tall trees.

There was another flour mill, Sharp's, by the road
opposite the gate of Cheeverstown but it, like Burke's, was
powered by the Watercourse. In the days when all the mills
were in operation the poor Dodder scarcely existed
between Firhouse and Rathfarnham until its tributary, the

Owendoher, renewed it.

At Templeogue, the suburbs which had been beginning to encroach on the river take over the scene. The cattle have long since left the pasture and all the many open spaces are under the control of County and City Councils. The remaining reaches of the Dodder belong to a different world.

Heron

CHAPTER 4

Parks and suburbs — where the wilderness survives

From Templeogue Bridge the Dodder flows for 6.3 kilometres through ever deepening suburbia, descending some 35 metres to Clonskeagh Bridge. A happy combination of precipitous banks with propensity for flooding kept houses and gardens at a respectable distance from the river throughout the 19th century. Speculative builders were slow to move in thereafter, with the result that great areas of green space survived until the 1940s when the authorities took their enlightened decision to preserve the greater part of what remained. So the valley remains a haven, rich in wildlife and unwittingly landscaped by the builders of five strictly functional mill-dams.

Bushes, terraces and wagtails

Whosoever wishes to follow the Dodder strictly from Templeogue Bridge must be well-shod and prepared to slither down a steep bank, to wade along the river bed. Private gardens stretch all the way to the cliff-top on both sides for a while, then comes the long, slightly sinuous green of the right bank, property of the County Council. Willows and hazels and other bushes were planted on the steep, higher slopes in the 1980s.

These steep slopes have been pushed about to some extent by building and landscaping operations, but a length of unspoiled ancient river bank remains, between the houses of Butterfield Grove and the car park of Rathfarnham Shopping Centre. It is almost vertical and is screened by blackthorn, hawthorn, elder and other bushes. Between this bank and the water the level ground forms one more of the terraces where the Dodder wandered before it began to cut downwards again. Underneath the grounds of Templeogue Tennis Club, the undercutting of the river is dramatically demonstrated by the broken wall which hangs dangerously out over the abyss.

On the left bank, the accessible valley begins again at the charming crescent of cottages rejoicing, surprise, surprise, in the name of Riverside Drive. From this point the banks are less steep and have been covered with lawn. The emplacement of boulders, mainly of granite, and building of retaining walls keeps the river within bounds and the general air of this stretch is of a very civilised valley.

Grey wagtails are particularly fond of it. Their colours are not quite as brilliant as the kingfisher's but I count them amongst the most beautiful of all the river birds: delicate and slender, coloured a soft grey on the upper parts and fresh lemon yellow below. Their movements are always a joy to watch: a deliberate walk punctuated by an occasional flutter into the air to snatch some passing insect; all the time their long tails gently bobbing. This ceaseless movement is a character of many birds which live by rivers or on the seashore and probably allows them to take to the air very quickly when the water splashes dangerously close.

The grey wagtails are very specialised birds, seldom seen at any distance from small rivers like the Dodder. The Liffey nearby is too big for them, nor do they like the seaside. In autumn the young birds scatter all over the place and pay brief visits to gardens, to lake shores and to the coast. But by winter nearly all have returned to the streams where they pair and set up exclusive territories Otters live here, too. In 1989 spraints were found at the Springfield Bridge and a little way downstream.

Grey wagtail

Faulting in the limestone

Just downstream of the concrete bridge which carries Springfield Avenue, the Dodder takes a very sharp and remarkable turn to the right, heading due east for a while. It is remarkable because the general trend of the hill slope is northwards down the flank of the Liffey valley and this

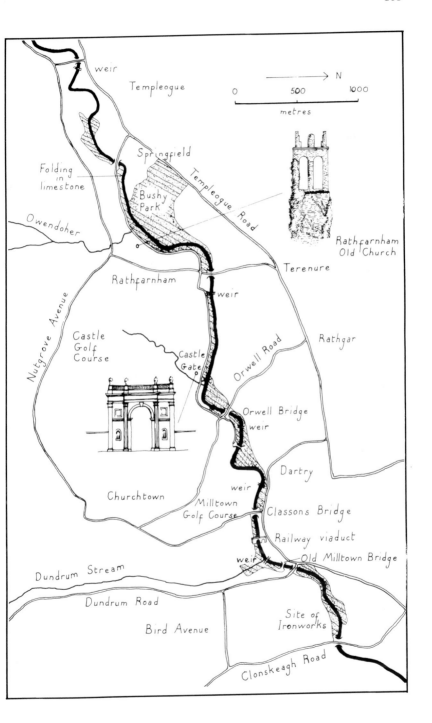

is the route which the nearby River Poddle takes. But both Liffey and Dodder have wills of their own and an entirely delightful way of ignoring convention.

There is no obvious impediment to the Dodder's northward path, but limestone outcrops begin to appear on the right bank just upstream of the bridge. It is possible that some now hidden rock on the left bank prevented the river from following the main slope. J. Selwyn Turner shows the Dodder all the way from Old Bawn to Rathfarnham following the trend of two fault lines near its left bank. One runs NE-SW, the other nearly east-west, joining the first a little to the west of Firhouse.

The effect of these faults was to bring older strata, the Cyathoxonia limestone, on the right bank into contact with younger strata, Posidonomya limestone, on the left. The younger rock may have been more resistant to erosion by the ancestral Dodder and so forced it to take a right turn. The modern river, cutting its way through glacial till, seldom makes contact with the bedrock hereabout but it may follow the direction of a pre-glacial valley carved when the nature of the rock would have had far more influence.

On the left bank, downstream of the bridge, a shaded footpath goes between the great grey limestone wall of Bushy Park and the unkempt thicket of the riverside, interrupted by small patches of lawn with newly-planted trees. An 'old quarry' is marked on the 1837 map in the ground to the east of Riverside Avenue, now covered in by the houses of Springfield Crescent. It seems very likely that this provided the stone both for the wall and for the building of Bushy Park house.

In places the even grey colour of the blocks in the wall is relieved by black bands two or three centimetres thick. This is chert, a deposit of silica which shares many of the properties of flint. The chert bands are typical of the Cyathoxonia limestones of the left bank. Chert was important to stone-age hunters and industrialists because it could be worked to produce good cutting edges. Flint from the chalk of County Antrim, and also available in smaller quantities on the Dublin seashore where the ice dropped it, is a superior material but the chert would have been cheaper and easier to come by for the ancestral dwellers by the Dodder.

The city boundary

Close to the bend in the river at the bridge, the boundary between city and county of Dublin, which runs southwards along Fortfield Road, meets the Dodder and from this point the river itself forms the dividing line. In practical terms this brings about a division of responsibilities for the two sides of the valley. Bushy Park is tended and loved by the Corporation Parks Department while the lawns on the right bank are under the equally devoted care of the County Council.

Limestone can be seen on both sides of the river. The first outcrop on the left bank is a low, almost level-topped slab. Outcrops on the right bank farther downstream are more interesting, showing the effects of folding and of 'thrusting' where the folds have been broken and pushed over one another. Two anticlines, the tips of inverted U shapes, lie close together showing where thrusting has

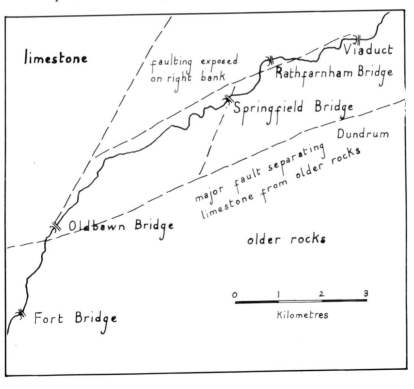

limestone

faulting exposed on right bank

Viaduct

Rathfarnham Bridge

Springfield Bridge

Dundrum

major fault separating limestone from older rocks

Oldbawn Bridge

older rocks

Fort Bridge

0   1   2   3
Kilometres

taken place. At this point the river is cutting across the line of a fault which runs towards the northeast.

The sediments which formed the limestone were deposited on the bed of a sea with beautifully clear water in a tropical climate. Ireland in those happy days was close to the equator. It is encouraging to bear that in mind when you look at the rock on a cold winter's day. Rivers from the nearby mountains flowed into the sea and pieces of the Wicklow granite have actually been found embedded in the limestone near Rathfarnham. I have looked and looked but so far failed to find any. More than a hundred million years passed between the emplacement of the granite in the Ordovician period and the deposition of the limestone in the Carboniferous. And nearly three hundred million years have gone by since the Carboniferous.

Towards the end of the Carboniferous the African continental plate moved against a united Europe and America. This time the crumpling of the rock took place along an east-west axis, but the little folds opposite Bushy Park do not follow this line. The faults on either side of the Dodder on the other hand are in keeping with the main trend. The shattering of strata by folding and faulting did not follow any simple pattern so there are plenty of faults out of line with the main ones. The major mountain building at this time took place well to the south and the upheavals are called Hercynian after the Hartz Mountains in Germany. The same folding accounts for the parallel ranges in the south of Ireland but it was generally weakening towards the north.

On the left bank, opposite the pair of anticlines, a stone arch in the high wall has been filled in. There were ponds and a water garden close to the house in the great days of Bushy Park and this arch may have been open to allow the water to return to the river.

A little way downstream on the right bank, the Owendoher joins the Dodder. This was the stream which restored the river in the worst days of the depredations of its waters perpetrated by Firhouse Weir. The water from the Owendoher made milling on the Dodder a possibility again about a mile lower down.

Willow and alder are the dominant bushes by the riverside. Besides the more common song birds, they are a

Winter sunshine in Dartry Park.

favourite haunt of long-tailed tits and goldcrests. The long-tailed tits may be seen anywhere on the Dodder downstream of the mountains, wonderful birds which would be the smallest in the land were it not for their tails, roughly equal in length to their tiny fluffy pink and black bodies. They generally travel in parties of five to ten, busily working over the slender branches hunting for insects. As they don't stay long in one place you can never be certain of meeting long-tailed tits but there is usually at least one party to every couple of miles of Dodder bank.

Bushy Park

On the other side of the wall was the splendid demesne of Bushy Park. A house was built there in 1700 by Arthur Bushe, Secretary to the Revenue Commissioners. Subsequently this house was either demolished or thoroughly rebuilt to make the existing Georgian building, modified by the addition of 19th-century windows on the ground floor.

In 1796 house and grounds were given as part of a dowry to Maria Wilkinson on her marriage to Robert Shaw. The 19th-century descendants, it is alleged, considered themselves too exalted for the company of George Bernard. The relationship was, in any case, tenuous. GBS was the grandson of a first cousin of the owner.

In the 20th century the Shaws sold off some of their estate as building land — it used to extend all the way to Terenure. But they continued to occupy the greater part of the demesne until 1951 when it was acquired by Dublin Corporation. Ultimately the house and 20 acres were sold by the Corporation in 1953 to the Religious of Christian Education who have kept a school there ever since. The remaining space, including most of the magnificent garden, is public property and beautifully maintained.

Within the park there is a strip of level ground surrounding the three ponds. This was the flood plain of the Dodder before its bed was lowered by the 19th-century Drainage Commissioners and it extends back to the steep bank where the river once flowed. Up above this the ground is a level expanse of lawn, playing fields and tennis courts, shaded by many splendid specimen trees. Jim Shannon's guide to the Bushy Park Trail gives an excellent account of these and other trees and their folklore.

There are two contrasting parts to the lower region of the park. Upstream, beech and other trees cast a dense shade. Indeed, beneath the beeches hardly any plants can grow and the bank when not carpeted with fallen leaves is bare. The ponds here are also shaded and seldom visited by water birds.

A sad little tea house survives in this part. It was built as a rural retreat for the Shaws to partake of tea in sylvan surroundings and decorated on the inside with patterns made from sea shells in the plaster. The shells are mainly cockles and were probably collected from the shore in Dublin Bay. Much of the plaster has fallen and taken the shells with it so that only traces remain of this very Victorian artistry.

The other part of the riverside park is bright and open, with fewer trees. The steep banks are covered with flowers: some with the St John's wort *Hypericum calycinum*, some with old man's beard which bears grey, hair-like fruits in winter, some with ivy. The lake is always busy with birds, above all with mallard which are very remarkable ducks in adapting themselves to tolerating and even using people for their own ends. What is exciting about mallard is that they are perfectly wild, free to fly wherever they please — but they find life easier in deepest suburbia.

They are the ducks which endear themselves to generations of small children in their insatiable appetites for breadcrumbs. Mallard deserve to be looked at closely. The ducks at first seem to be drab, but they display a subtle pattern of shades of brown and when they spread their wings a pair of brilliant metallic blue patches with white borders appear. The drakes have bright, if slightly incongruous, colouring with their bottle-green heads and white collars. But they too have delicate patterns: pencil-thin lines of white and grey on their wings, concealing big blue badges the same as the ducks'. And in spring the flotillas of newly hatched ducklings appear, coloured in shades of yellow and brown, bursting with activity as they scamper across the water hunting for insects.

Swans visit the lake and sometimes stay to breed.

Moorhens are permanent residents and black-headed gulls gather there at any time of year — but in winter their heads are white. Coots are confined to the lake because they are very choosy about their habitat. The water must be exactly the right depth to allow weed to grow on the bottom and there must be little or no current. So the Dodder outside the park is too swift for coots and the lakes in Glenasmole too deep.

Rathfarnham and its bridge

The land by the riverside on the right bank downstream of the Owendoher was pasture up to the end of the 1950s, the only dwellings being the two little rows of houses at the bottom of Church Lane. The Dodder used to wander more freely, over to the steep bank below the village of Rathfarnham and the Georgian house Ashfield on the hill, surrounded by trees. Ashfield in former times stood, like Bushy Park, in the midst of park land and extensive gardens. Then came the need to sell much of the estate to speculative builders. Fortunately, by the 1950s, the decision had been taken to preserve open spaces along the river and the new houses were kept at a respectful distance. Indeed, the area is now much more accessible than in the times of private ownership when the only approach was under Rathfarnham Bridge.

The medieval church of Rathfarnham stands on the hillside in an old cemetery. Little remains of it but a gable with two arched openings in which bells once hung. Nearby is the church built to replace it, with the aid of a grant of £400 from the Irish Parliament in 1783. The foundation stone was laid in 1784 and the church was opened in the following year.

Rathfarnham medieval church

The building of the road along the Dodder led to a certain amount of confining of the river by concrete retaining walls and the County Council's treatment of the right bank has been to transform most of it to a well-kept lawn. Less exciting for naturalists than something more wildernessy, it does provide passing motorists with an uninterrupted view of the willows and wild flowers on the left bank and the magnificent trees of Bushy Park. The lawn is far from barren. The short grass is an ideal hunting ground for many birds: black-headed gulls, mistle thrushes, song thrushes and blackbirds, starlings, jackdaws and rooks and occasional hooded crows all like to dig for worms and insect larvae.

The next bridge is a graceful single arch faced with limestone. Pádraig Pearse crossed it many times on the road between St Enda's and the city, and it was renamed Pearse Brothers' Bridge. Bridges came and went at Rathfarnham. The first historical record is of the, perhaps limited, munificence of John Douce of St Audoen's parish who bequeathed, by his will dated 1381, the sum of one mark towards the cost of construction. Gerard Boate wrote in 1645:

> To go from Dublin to Rafernam, one passeth this River upon a wooden bridge; the which although it be high and strong, nevertheless hath severall times been quite broke, and carried away through the violence of sudden floods; although at other times, and when the Brook doth only carry its ordinary water, a child of five years may easily and without danger wade through it; and a tall man on horseback riding underneath it, not being able to reach it; in the great floods the water many times riseth so high that it doth not only touch, but floweth quite over the bridge.

After Boate's time a bridge was built in 1659 and destroyed in due course. Its replacement went in 1728 and the next one in June 1754, carried away by floods following the heaviest rain known for years. Its successor was also destroyed. But the Dodder finally admitted defeat and the bridge erected in 1765 still stands. During the Second World War tank barriers were built above it and the sides of the arch below were drilled to take explosive charges in the event of invasion. Widening and rebuilding took place after the war. The new structure, on the upstream side, is of reinforced concrete but the shape remains the same and the masonry was beautifully restored.

A dye works near the bridge was in 1752 owned by Mrs

Elizabeth Fisher and this may have been succeeded by the extensive building named Ely Cloth Factory marked on the 1837 map upstream of the bridge on the right bank. No trace remains of the factory which lay downstream of a mill standing where the Owendoher meets the Dodder. This may be the cloth mill at Rathfarnham, owned by John Higginson, mentioned in 1641 when, in the words of Elrington Ball:

> The caretaker and his family were assailed with shots and great stones, and the caretaker only saved his life by escaping through the sluices of the mill and taking refuge in the Castle.

Foxes, shrews, badgers and butter

Downstream of the bridge, houses with back gardens keep wanderers away from the river for a while. On the left bank they go as far as the weir, on the right for about 100 metres where a comfortably low wall separates footpath from river. In the 19th century there was a line of trees above the river on the right bank, their place now taken by Lower Dodder Road. This shows that the river by then was confined to its fairly narrow course. Behind the houses of Lower Dodder Road and the parallel Dodder Park Road, a steep bank rises marking the outer edge of a former river terrace. The houses of Lower Dodder Road were built in the 1930s just a little before the Abercrombie Plan for Dublin in 1941 recommended the development of a linear park.

Rathfarnham Weir goes straight across the river and used to feed a millrace on the left bank. A stone arch immediately downstream supported a sluice gate which controlled the overflow. The mill race ran close to the main stream, at the bottom of the cliff of glacial till. Although the mill was long-forgotten, the stream held water as late as the 1960s.

The path of the millrace is now wonderfully overgrown. Sycamore, beech and ash and occasional yews and lime trees grow on the upper parts: alder and willow on the lower. The ground cover is heliotrope, butterbur and alexanders. Sparrow hawks nested there in 1989 and probably do so every year. Access to the left bank, where this small forest grows, is faintly inconvenient. The right bank has a riverside footpath and a very good case can be made for leaving the woodland on the left just as it is. In summer it forms a great green curtain, hiding the housing of Bushy Park Road. In winter much greenery remains and the browns of the tree trunks are relieved by the purple of birch twigs and great splashes of orange and willow stems. Early in the new year, pale yellow-green hazel catkins mark the first whisperings of spring.

The orange stems belong to the variety of white willow called *vitellina*. Unknown as a wild tree, its history goes back at the very least to 1623 and it may well have been grown by the ancient Romans. Most, probably all, of the Dodder vitellinas were planted as ornamental trees. The twigs, however, are tough and pliable and were used like string so the variety was often grown for utilitarian purposes. Weeping willows are also plentiful by the lower Dodder. The Latin name of the species is *babylonica*, given by the great Swedish naturalist Linnaeus. His idea was beautiful: Psalm 137 begins 'By the rivers of Babylon, there we sat down, yea we wept when we remembered Zion. We hanged our harps upon the willows in the midst thereof.' Unfortunately, modern research shows that willow is a mis-translation and the trees in question were poplars. But what matter, it is one of the most beautiful of trees and, if not from Babylon itself, the variety comes from somewhere in the romantic east. And some of the finest specimens anywhere can be seen in the valley of the Dodder.

Butterbur, a plant with enormous, rhubarb-like leaves, is a native species which thrives on the banks of rivers and effectively shuts out all other flowers by casting a dense shade. Alexanders, especially noticeable in winter when its shiny, dark green leaves stand out, was a garden plant in the 17th century, its young leaves used in salads. It had already run wild early in the 18th century when Caleb Threlkeld in 1727 noted that:

It grows under our Hedges in the Ditches, and especially on a small Bushy Hillock near *Crumlin* Church

and added that it

Butterbur

was formerly blanched in our gardens and eaten with oil, salt and pepper, but of late has given way to Cellery.

Foxes inhabit the woods along the mill stream and elsewhere in the suburban valley here. Badgers have been seen recently and probably have setts somewhere well hidden in the thickets. One fox a long time ago had the temerity to dine on butter delivered to the doorstep of the editor of *The Irish Times*. Others have a less distinguished diet but they undoubtedly thrive in the region. A little way upstream of Rathfarnham Weir lives a cat which brings pygmy shrews as an offering to its mistress. There are probably many other shrew-catching cats in the valley but this one constituted a definite scientific record of the presence of both species.

The kingfisher

Kingfishers live on this stretch and used to have nesting burrows on the right bank about half way between Rathfarnham Weir and the castle gate. They were concreted over some time ago, probably unwittingly. As in the case of the sand martins, kingfishers are constrained to nest in rather rare patches of the river bank where the sand has exactly the right consistency. Anyway, they have found other sites and continue to be as plentiful in the valley as they were when I first saw them fifty years ago.

Kingfisher

The brilliant blue or green plumage of the kingfisher is well known and a flash of bright colour is as much as a casual onlooker ever sees of the bird. Surprisingly, the blue-green back and chestnut breast keep a kingfisher well hidden when it perches on a leafy branch and remains perfectly still. So it is a bird which can quite easily be passed by unnoticed.

Giraldus Cambrensis who wrote of the wildlife of Ireland in the 12th century made a very remarkable observation about them. He stated that the kingfishers of Ireland had black and white plumage rather than bright colours. Without doubt he was describing the dipper. Apparently he had never seen kingfishers in Ireland and it may be that they had not reached the country by his time.

The Castle Gate

The triumphal arch near the right bank was one of the two gateways to Rathfarnham Castle. Built in the 1770s by Henry, Viscount Ely who was responsible for much of the finest interior decoration of the Castle, it was still not only a functioning, but an inhabited gate house in the 1940s. When Dodder Park Road was built it left the gateway on a little green island bordered by three roads. Maples, birch and willow have been planted in front of it. This little park, incidentally, is County Council property while Orwell Park across the river is part of the City.

The gate house was a splendid building in its day, of neatly cut granite blocks. Now it looks a little sad: windows blocked in, the urns from the two wings and one from the top vanished together with one pilaster from the balustrade. The elaborate wrought iron gate is a little rusted, but to this day effectively bars the progress of the populace through the arch — even though the passage leads to nowhere but the other side.

Behind the gateway lies a valley where the avenue to the castle once ran. Nearby a small tributary stream flows close to Woodside Drive from the Castle Golflinks. It goes under

Rathfarnham Castle Gate

the road in a culvert and enters the Dodder through an inelegant rectangular opening in the concrete retaining wall downstream of the footbridge. Weston Joyce in 1903 described the valley as 'densely wooded' and some fine old trees remain. Most have been removed over the years, making room for houses and a caravan park.

Orwell Park

Opposite the castle gate the footbridge was built in 1950 to give access to the riverside park which was developed on land acquired from the Bewley family — whose Jersey cattle grazed there and supplied milk for the cafés. Otter spraints and footprints — more properly known as 'seals' — were found near the footbridge in 1989. A quarry pond, ten metres deep, close to the bridge was filled with tennis courts when the High School moved to the estate. The mill stream flowed above and behind the quarry pond and then along the base of the cliff which curves away from the present bed of the main river. The park occupies the flood plain in between.

This is marked as a 'drying green' on old maps and was protected from floods by the long dyke which runs a little way back from the river for most of the way to Orwell Bridge. In spite of it, the field used to be flooded periodically until the crest of Rathfarnham Weir was lowered in the 1930s. The dyke has been cut or worn away in places and, close to the footbridge, the lime kiln which now serves as a shed was built into it. You can peep in behind the locked door to see the brick-arch structure within the kiln. Maybe some day the unprepossessing door will be replaced with a gate so that people can enjoy an easier view of the interior.

Blocks of limestone from the quarry were burned in the kiln to form the dangerously corrosive 'quicklime' (calcium oxide). The quicklime was then placed in heaps on the ground so that the rain could soak it, slaking its thirst and yielding the hydroxide, 'slaked lime'. In this form it could be handled more safely and spread on the ground to improve the soil. Nowadays limestone is pulverised mechanically and supplied as 'ground limestone' so the kilns are rapidly disappearing from the countryside. Since the park was opened forty years ago, the lime kiln has changed its status from a commonplace object to an important relic of industrial archaeology.

Between dyke and river some alders and hawthorn survive and weeping willows were planted in the 1970s. On the inner side of the bank, on the far side of the lime kiln, a very old willow leans out over the green. It may have adopted this peculiar stance to get out of the shade cast by the sycamore and ash on the mound behind it.

A paddling pool with a concrete submarine was built when the park was first opened to the public in 1950. It has a special personal interest because it was the place where, at about the age of ten, I made my first encounter with an eel. The pond was half empty and the eel apparently had exhausted itself in trying to escape. It was too weak to be slippery so I was able to carry it back to the safety of the river. Pool and submarine were demolished in 1990, the stagnant water being too unhygienic for the clean infancy of modern times. Eels still inhabit this stretch of the Dodder: a remarkable feat since they have to climb several waterfalls to reach it.

Across the river from the park, the right bank is a high cliff of glacial till, surmounted by the 19th-century red-brick

The curved weir at Orwell Bridge.

building of the Church of Ireland Theological College. In common with most of the other old buildings, it stands above the valley, beyond the reach of the highest floods.

The drying green behind the dyke was associated with Waldron's calico printing mill which had ceased operation by the time Robert Mallet was writing in 1844. This mill stood close to Orwell Road. At a later stage the water was used to drive Rathgar Sawmill, owned by Locke and Woods. Remnants, including a fallen chimney, were visible up to the 1950s.

The mill stream ran at the far side of the playing fields, driving a wheel close to the present day tennis courts. Some of the mill buildings remain, partly modernised as dwellings and partly used as a garage. A wooden bridge was built there by Patrick Waldron who lived on the high ground of the left bank in Rathgar House. His bridge was succeeded by a stone one which has been completely replaced in concrete, a tragic removal of an old stone arch. But it has the redeeming feature of footpaths on both banks so that you no longer have to cross Orwell Road to continue your journey down the river.

A little way upstream of Orwell Bridge on the left bank stands the new flood gauge and little concrete house where the recording meter works. New because the Hurricane Charlie floods overtopped its predecessor, it had to be built higher in an effort to measure accurately the depth of water at the greatest conceivable flood.

The Step Dodder

The next stretch, according to my family usage, was the Step Dodder, so called because the only access until the new bridge was built was by a twisted narrow stone stairway. The steps have been straightened and widened but an old wall by the river, of limestone blocks with granite coping, has survived. A small, scarcely visible, piece of roadside furniture stands at the beginning of the iron fence: a granite plinth with a bronze medallion announcing that this was the boundary of the Township of Rathmines in 1847. Together with the Township of Pembroke, Rathmines surrendered its independence to the Dublin Corporation in 1930. Beyond lay the rural fastnesses of the County of Dublin which have since been beaten westwards to Fortfield Road. The boundary, however, remains, separating the municipal wards of Terenure to the west and Rathmines and Rathgar to the east.

Dartry Park

The steep bank of glacial till comes close to the riverside, only just leaving room for the footpath but moving away a little at the next weir, one of the most beautiful, with a gently curved sill over which the water plunges in an even white curtain. Mallet described it as:

> a sound piece of masonry, but greatly undermined by the scouring away of the bed of the river, which is at least four feet below the original apron.

The millrace ran along the base of the cliff to the left but most of it has been filled in. Up above the little footbridge stands a particularly good exposure of the glacial till. Just below a Scots pine and a holm oak the cliff is too steep for any vegetation to cover it. The typical unsorted nature of glacial deposits can be seen clearly: a matrix of rather clayey material with big, angular lumps of limestone sticking out.

On the right bank there is another wide valley. This one seems to be devoid of any stream and, rather than a tributary valley, may be a low area between two high bluffs. On this dangerously low-lying ground dozens of dwellings with gardens have been packed in below the cliff. High above them, large 19th-century houses look down from secure and dry positions. The lower houses of Orwell Gardens suffer once in every fifty years or so when the Dodder gives vent to a fit of rage and escapes from the concrete walls in which the drainage engineers seek to confine her.

The steep cliff comes back to the riverside once more, just downstream of Orwell Gardens and the wilderness asserts itself again. An ancient retaining wall of limestone blocks protects the base of the cliff from erosion. A series of low concrete weirs has been placed across the river to provide pools for the trout.

One of the nine limestone arches of the Milltown Viaduct.

At the weir on the left bank the ground is level, except for a long dyke, now covered over with grass and something of a hedge of elder bushes. This forms Dartry Park, leased by a Murphy family to the Corporation for 999 years from 1st January 1949. Where the lawn beside the river has been cut away, the soil beneath is fine gravel, not glacial clay. The gravel has been deposited by the river at times of flood rather than dumped by the ice.

This, like Orwell Park, and Orwell Gardens, is an 'incised meander' of the river. In the days of its freedom the Dodder cut into the glacial till on the outer side of each curve, the curves gradually becoming bigger and embracing an increasingly large area of almost level alluvial soil. The gravel deposited by the river is largely derived from limestone. It drains easily and provides plenty of lime so that a rich soil develops — as witnessed by the green grass and the vigorous hawthorns, blackthorns and elder. The enlargement of the curve does not go on for ever. Ultimately, the river in a high flood abandons the old bed, cutting off or incising the meander so that the old bank is left far from the water's edge. Retaining walls and houses nowadays put an end to these wayward habits.

Across the level ground, behind the row of cypresses, traces of the millrace have survived the landscaping. It led in behind the houses at the end of the park, passed under the road and drove a colossal water wheel which was removed in 1950. Its left hand mounting can still be seen opposite the modern part of Messrs North's premises and the last remnant of the mill pond across the road is gradually disappearing under a heap of garden rubbish.

In 1844 this was Willan's cloth mill. Mallet mentioned that, a little above it:

> the overhanging clay banks of the river are in a state of rapid and serious degradation.

It must have been to counteract this that the stone retaining wall was built on the right bank. The water wheel was still there, though unused, when the premises had changed from a cloth mill to the Dartry Dye Works. Great vats of dye stood in a long, low shed on the right bank, approached by the girder bridge. Cloth is woven once again on the left bank.

Beneath the girder bridge the water begins to flow silent and deep once more as it approaches the weir below South Hill. Moorhen and mallard enjoy the gentle flow and grey wagtails hunt by the bank. Access to the river is blocked for a little way by the factory buildings but the weir is accessible from the road on the left bank. The millrace led off from the left-hand end of the weir but has been filled in by the tarmac footpath. It can just be traced there, partly filled with soil and overgrown with brambles, making its way behind the three park benches. It ends in a stone arch which once upon a time was the opening of a culvert to bring the stream beneath the road. The mill race came to the surface again where the great railway viaduct stands.

Classon's Bridge

Classon's Bridge, downstream of the weir, is marked on the 1837 map. It had three round arches of limestone masonry which you may still see if you go down below. They were brutally encased in reinforced concrete when the bridge was rebuilt in 1928. The four iron lamp standards go a little way towards atoning for this savagery. Spraints were found there in 1989 together with a smear of mucus which the otter uses to define its territory.

The left bank at Classon's Bridge has a narrow strip of green between road and river. Where it slopes steeply horsetails abound. The demesnes on the left were South Hill and Nullamore: South Hill has been engulfed by housing. Nullamore, now a residence for university students, has survived as a house with extensive grounds. The Dodder down below has been rather fiercely constricted between high retaining walls.

Mallet records only Moore's cloth mill at this point, but there were many more before his time — the name of Milltown goes back to the 14th century. James Hegarty mentions five:

During the eighteenth century there were at Milltown two corn mills, an iron mill, a paper factory, and a saw mill owned by James Classon, from whom Classon's Bridge is named.

Traces of some of these could be seen in the Dublin Laundry in the 1940s but the site now is abandoned and overgrown — perhaps when the Corporation sets to work on its planned park, somebody may unearth and preserve the last remnants of the mills.

The right bank has a great, rolling sward of lawn where the housing estates are kept firmly away from the riverside. There once was a quarry a little way downstream of the bridge but it has long since been filled in. Bare limestone appears in the river bed on both sides of the bridge. Sometimes oystercatchers come to the lawn to dig for worms.

Oystercatcher

The Milltown Viaduct

Downstream at this point stands one of the most spectacular man-made features of the Dodder valley, the great viaduct of the Dublin-Dundrum railway whose life began in 1846. Known in due course as the 'Harcourt Street Line', the railway was closed in 1958. The reasons why the perpetrators of the demise of the railway did not also do away with the viaduct remain concealed in some filing system. Probably it was cheaper to let it stay in place. What was once a purely functional railway bridge now stands as a magnificent memorial to the skill of 19th-century engineers and stone masons.

The facing is of rectangularly cut blocks of limestone. White streaks, looking like spilt paint, are the marks of lime leached from the mortar. Little pencil-sized stalactites hang from the arches, again formed by water percolating through the mortar, dissolving the lime and depositing it once more as the droplets evaporate. Stalactites need relatively calm air to develop so there are many more of them on the east side of the bridge than on the west since they have an element of shelter from the prevailing south-westerlies.

The wasteland downstream of the viaduct on the left bank is over-run by buddleias. With the aid of numerous nettles they provide a wonderful habitat for several species of butterflies, the finest of them being the red admiral. Buddleias, for a long time confined to gardens, had a population explosion and for twenty years and more have become the dominant shrub all over the derelict sites of Dublin's fair city. This butterfly habitat once was occupied by the Dublin Laundry whose extensive buildings are now reduced to the tall red-brick chimney. The tailrace of one of the many mills can just be made out immediately downstream of the viaduct.

The river takes a sharp bend to the left at the laundry site, bringing into view some old houses, two-storey and cottage, built for mill-workers in the 19th century. The left bank once was a great walled orchard and will, no doubt, be brought back to parkland at some stage. On the right bank, surrounded by nettle and hogweed, an iron pipe reaches heavenward, springing from a cast-iron urn which bears the inscription:

R. No.1 R.D.C. Tonge and Taggart Ltd. Dublin 1911.

It is an air vent for the discreetly concealed main sewer which runs along the Dodder valley in the general direction of Ringsend.

Close to this solitary column the Dundrum Stream enters the Dodder through a culvert. It is a sad stream, even in 1990 having defied the efforts of the authorities to free it from pollution. So the waters which it adds to the Dodder are all too often grey and malodorous. The problem has been to trace all the sewerage outlets from old homesteads.

The ground around the next weir is a rather unattractive tip-heap with willow herb, burdock and many other interesting weeds. The weir itself is dilapidated but some of its sluice gates remain in position and there is good stonework in places: definitely scope for a satisfying restoration job some day. The weir probably owes its existence to a natural waterfall of limestone, now hidden beneath the masonry. An outcrop of limestone forms the left bank just downstream and below it lies a series of gently dipping beds of rock.

The 1937 map names the weir Millmount and shows buildings upstream and downstream of it. They have almost disappeared and the millrace has been filled in with rubbish. You can just trace it from the iron sluice gate beside the weir, running perilously close to the retaining wall on the right bank. It ran under an arch which still survives in the old bridge and then made its way beneath the new one, but no trace of that can be seen. The road from Dundrum formerly took a bend to the left and crossed the Dodder at the abandoned stone bridge which, with its pedestrian refuge, looks almost like a castle.

Blue mills and balsam

A pleasant row of old houses, one-storey and two-storey, stands above the river and behind it, clambering over the steep hillside, are the ruins of yet another mill, marked as a Blue Mill on the 1837 map. Blueing was a process in making cloth pure white. To the right of the last house in the row there is a stone arch which probably marks the position of the tailrace. This mill was the lowest of several powered by the Dundrum stream and not by the Dodder.

The gravel islands and the banks of the river here provide wild flowers in plenty: monkey flower down by the river and balsam on the banks. Balsam, like the monkey flower, is another naturalised species. It comes from the Himalayas but was not known as a Dublin plant in Nathaniel Colgan's time in 1904. By the 1930s it had appeared in the county but took many more years to reach the Dodder — nobody seems to have made a definite record of the arrival. By the 1980s balsam had become one of the most common species on the riverside, a very striking plant with red stems and big bulbous pink flowers.

On the left bank below the Milltown Bridge the Corporation parkland is an expanse of lawn beloved of black-headed gulls. Across the river on a small hill Clonskeagh Castle, embellished with 19th-century battlements, stands surrounded by tall beech trees. The river is very constricted but the series of little weirs provides sufficient depth of water to attract a permanent community of mallard to it. The lawn ends in a narrow lane which runs between the river and a cluster of houses of various shapes and sizes, including an old terrace of red-brick cottages.

Past the cottages the lane gives access to a dismal

deserted field, inhabited by the skeletons of cars. Those who rejoice in such displays of waste must hasten to enjoy it while it lasts. Recently acquired by the Corporation the area is due for corrective treatment. Meanwhile there is an interesting little cliff of pale brown glacial till, standing on top of an outcrop partly of limestone, partly of shale. Above it an heroic sycamore survives with the determination so characteristic of the species. Its roots cling to the vertical cliff face, reminiscent of the hands of a rock-climber. The cliff, though high above the river now, was undercut by it in the past.

Clonskeagh and its ironworks

The right bank is occupied by the last of the County Council's parks, lying between the wall of the demesne of Clonskeagh Castle and the river. It makes a secluded walk, shaded by the old trees within the grounds. The millrace from Millmount has been obliterated near the

Balsam

bridge, its last trace being a pair of small stone arches near the ground in the outer wall of Milltown Grove apartment blocks.

The bed of the river in many places here is bare limestone, an unusual feature because lowland river beds normally are coated with gravel or silt. Possibly the narrow constrictions of the Dodder between its retaining walls increase the speed of the current and lead to a scouring action which keeps the stone swept clean. A little garden with brick walls and cotoneaster has been made where a stone tunnel on the right marks the path of the old mill stream. The tunnel once was a bridge over the millrace and it carried the footpath up and along by the wall above.

Below this the millrace crossed a gully by a stone aqueduct which still stands, a large arch by the riverside

An old willow at Rathfarnham.

looking rather meaningless now: neatly built of limestone, its dark, cool and damp interior inhabited by a single hart's tongue fern. About 150 metres downstream of the garden the millrace widened into a large pond, now completely filled in. Arthur Brooks, who lived in Clonskeagh for some years from 1914, remembered swans, moorhen and dabchicks in the pond, and cuckoos, corncrakes and skylarks nearby.

If you look very carefully you may find a slag heap farther downstream on the bank. That is all that remains of Clonskeagh Iron Works, a factory whose ancestors go back as far as 1316 when Henry Jackson owned a mill there. For many years before the garden was finally created, the site was derelict and occupied by one citizen in a mobile home. He had ingeniously chosen his parking place on the border between city and county so that when one authority required him to move on, he could leave its jurisdiction with a minimum of effort.

Rebuilt to carry heavier traffic, the graceful curved arch of Clonskeagh Bridge was copied in reinforced concrete and the faces were restored with neat panels of granite. Here the river turns northwards and the County Borough Boundary continues to follow it for just a little way, turning to the west at the footbridge below the waterfall. So at this point the Dodder becomes a truly urban river, flowing for its final two miles through Dublin's Fair City.

TOP: The lakes of Glenasmole and the suburbs of Dublin.
ABOVE: The old Milltown Bridge.

TOP: View upstream towards Oldbawn Bridge. The low wall of boulders protects the park from erosion.
ABOVE: The flood-plain of the Dodder, once a drying green, forming part of Orwell Park.

TOP: In Dartry Park; the low concrete weir in the foreground is one of a series built to make pools for trout.
LEFT: The splendid weeping willow at Orwell Bridge.

ABOVE: The footbridge to Orwell Park. The trees on the right follow the path of an old millrace below a cliff of glacial till.
OPPOSITE: The viaduct of the Harcourt Street Line and the chimney of the Dublin Laundry.

A lamp on Ballsbridge.

TOP: The pumping station at London Bridge.
ABOVE: Ringsend Bridge, built in 1803.

Salmon nets at the mouth of the Dodder.

CHAPTER 5

In Dublin's Fair City

At Clonskeagh Bridge the Dodder is 18 metres above sea level and 3.7 km from its mouth on the South Wall of the Liffey. Until it meets the head of the tide at Ballsbridge, the character of the river is similar to the preceding stretch, a lowland stream interrupted by weirs where the remnants of control sluices and millraces may still be seen. Everything changes at Ballsbridge. In the first place the tide takes command. Twice a day the river changes from a relatively deep waterway to a narrow stream flowing between sandbanks — as it always did. But this is also the region where the human hand has exerted an influence to equal that of the Glenasmole dam. Stone walls confine the Dodder all the way to the sea, so that only on extremely rare occasions can the water spread far and wide over its now hidden delta.

Beech Hill and Beaver Row

Shops and buildings on the left bank prevent access to the footpath which goes by the river nearly all the way from Clonskeagh to Anglesey Bridge. A wall of concrete blocks a little too high for civilised folk to climb with decorum — if too low to discourage one single vandal — blocks the upstream end of the path. So the journey downstream must be continued on the right bank along the footpath first of Beech Hill and then of Beaver Row.

A house called Beech Hill is marked on the 1837 map but the site is submerged beneath office blocks and factories and few beech trees remain. Beaver Row dates at least to 1816 and its charming one and two storey houses have a respectable air of antiquity. There were mills on the left bank and quarries on the right and the houses were originally built for the workers.

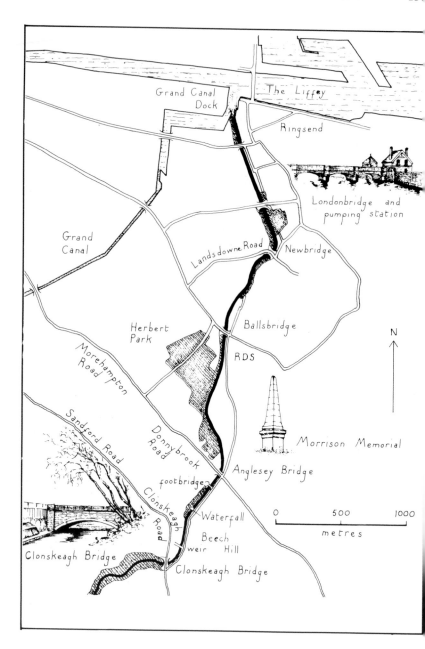

The rocky bottom of the Dodder becomes more and more significant between Clonskeagh Bridge and Angelsey Bridge. The rock strata here are part of the Cyathoxonia beds (page 104) but older than those between Old Bawn and Rathfarnham. They extend as far as Anglesey Bridge and then the river passes through the lower and older limestone strata known as the Calp. The word 'calp' is not found in English dictionaries but *calk* is the word for 'lime' in modern Scandinavian languages. Calp therefore may be a local Dublin term of Viking descent.

There are two substantial waterfalls, the upper one now completely encased in the stonework of a weir. The dominant feature of the left bank is the Smurfit papermill, descendant of a long line of establishments using the water power. In the 19th century it was Portis's iron mill. Smurfit's now discharges all its waste legitimately into the sewerage system and the Dodder flows by uncontaminated. The mills use a certain amount of Dodder water for their processing but no longer avail of its power. They recycle waste paper to produce cardboard which is made into corrugated packaging elsewhere.

The First Cataract

Immediately downstream of the weir, the river begins to form the next millpond, held back by masonry which fills in the gaps and raises the level of the First Cataract of the Dodder usually, if more prosaically, known as the Beaver Row Waterfall. Not quite as imposing as its counterpart on the Nile, this is a real rock waterfall, not just a weir, a massive outcrop of limestone, gently folded near the left bank. Seatrout and salmon come this far up the Dodder and sometimes manage to mount the falls to go on upstream.

All that remains of the waterworks associated with the fall is a green-painted sluice, its gate still in place on the left bank. The millstream is mostly filled in but can be traced within the iron railings on the higher of the two footpaths until it disappears from view at a brick arch down at the bottom of a rather lost-looking wall. The millstream parted company with the river and flowed for about 250 metres in the direction of Donnybrook where Hugh McGuirk and

Co. operated large saw mills beside the fair green.

Across the river are the futuristic buildings of the Riverview Racket and Fitness Club, together with the long-established printing works. The footpath of Beaver Row, between the two weirs, passes from county to city, the boundary marked by a rather unimpressive concrete slab.

Donnybrook Fair

In 1204 King John wrote to Meiler FitzHenry, Justiciary of Ireland, directing him to build Dublin Castle but adding:

> We WILL also, that there be a Fair at Donniburn annually to continue for eight days on the feast of the Invention of the Holy Cross.

A subsequent letter granted a licence for the holding of Donnybrook Fair each year on the vigil, day and morrow of the day of the Invention of the Holy Cross (3rd May) and for five days thereafter. The profits from the tolls for the vigil and the day were granted to the Archbishop of Dublin.

In the course of time the season of the fair was extended to fifteen days and the date was advanced as the century wore on, so that a goodly list of saints and martyrs enjoyed a period of honour: in 1241 the feast of the Translation of St Thomas the Martyr, in 1279 the Translation of St Benedict the Abbot (in July) and finally to the Decollation of St John the Baptist, on the 29th of August. So it moved from Spring Show to Horse Show time.

The fair green is shown in John Taylor's map of 1816, a strip of land along the left bank of the river both upstream and downstream of Donnybrook Road. Eglinton Road and the more recent Jefferson House occupy much of the ground and there is no trace of McGuirk's Mill. For nearly six hundred years the fair flourished, without doubt a marvellous summer outing for the poor, with all the food and drink and entertainments of whatever period. It was also an important occasion for the more serious business of trading in livestock. The traditional ballad gives a comprehensive picture of the range of activities.

The mason does come with his line and his plumb,
The sawyer and carpenter, brothers in chips.
There are carvers and gilders and all sorts of builders
With soldiers from barracks and sailors from ships.
There's confectioners, cooks and printers of books,
There stampers of linen and weavers repair.
There widows and maids and all sorts of trades,
Go join in the humours of Donnybrook Fair.

There's tinkers and nailers and beggars and tailors,
And singers of ballads and girls of the sieve.
With barrack street rangers, the known ones and strangers
And many that no one can tell how they live.
There's horsemen and walkers and likewise fruit hawkers,
And swindlers the devil himself that would dare.
With pipers and fiddlers and dandies and diddlers
All set in the humours of Donnybrook Fair.

'Tis there are dogs dancing, and wild beasts a prancing,
With neat bits of painting in red, yellow and gold;
Toss players and scramblers and showmen and gamblers,
Pickpockets in plenty, both of young and old.
There are brewers and bakers and jolly shoemakers,
With butchers and porters, and men that cut hair.
There are mountebanks grinning, while others are sinning,
To keep up the humours of Donnybrook Fair.

But it was all too much for the morality of the 19th century.
The tradition of more than six hundred years was brought
to an end by the authorities who felt the populace were
over-indulging themselves.

Elrington Ball wrote eloquently in favour of the ban:

The far-famed fair of Donnybrook was throughout the
eighteenth century, and down to the year 1855, when it was
abolished, the annual carnival of the Dublin populace. It
has formed the theme of innumerable ballads and humor-
ous descriptions, and it would be well if history could
confirm the account which they give of a scene of light-
hearted gaiety. This, however, truth does not permit. All
references in local literature indicate that the fair was the

The weir at Beaver Row and Smurfit papermill.

occasion of drunkenness, riot and moral degradation which were a disgrace to Ireland, and it would serve no useful purpose to enter more fully into particulars of revels, the abolition of which was a service to civilization.

Eminently respectable suburbs spread over the scene of past revelry — one can't help wondering whether the excesses of exuberance were really so bad, or did a gathering of 'the populace' simply threaten to depress the value of the Victorian houses? Laurence O'Dea gives a detailed history of the Fair which makes it clear that Elrington Ball exaggerated the low side. Certainly there were occasions when the celebrations and fights led to serious problems. But a number of contemporary observers, both tourists and Dublin journalists, reported on fairs which passed off with no serious incidents. It seems very likely that, had the authorities wished to do so, they could have kept the occasion entirely under control.

The reports of the time make two important points: first that neither the authorities nor the local landowners were making any money from the fair, second that the emancipated clergy, in particular one Reverend P J Nowlan, regarded the gathering as an occasion of sin. So it died and Father Nowlan and his followers shortly afterwards built the church which stands on the right bank, overlooking the scene of a sinful past. They saw it as something of an atonement.

The river bank below the waterfall is the latest to be made accessible as part of the linear park, its paths being spread with gravel and much of the jungle removed. It is a lovely little backwater, approached by a lattice girder footbridge supported by a vertical iron pillar. Protected from the movement of the traffic by the river and from its noise by the gentle roar of the waterfall, you can sit and dream of revels of long ago. Herons go fishing there and grey wagtails hunt busily by the banks. Sometimes a kingfisher comes to sit immobile on a low-hanging branch above the water.

The stone wall on the right bank rests on rock outcrops in places. Much of the outcropping material is massive grey limestone. Some of the rock at this point is shale, layered rather than massive. The pure limestone was laid down in bright and clear salt water. Shale is an estuarine deposit formed from silt brought down the mountains by ar ancestral Dodder: not a direct ancestor because the entire Carboniferous seaside came to be buried for many million: of years beneath a blanket of chalk and other strata. These were worn away again in the Tertiary Era over the last sixty million years when Ireland as we know it began to be formed.

Anglesey Bridge and Arthur Morrison

The twentieth century returns with a vengeance where Anglesey Bridge carries the incessant traffic of the Bray Road. The river was crossed by a ford until 1741 when the first bridge was built, only to be destroyed by flood six months later. The present, rather severe, structure was built in 1832 and bears the date in very handsome letters, together with the name Anglesey. Henry Richard Paget, Marquis of Anglesey was Lord Lieutenant at the time.

Father Nowlan's Sacred Heart Church, designed by Pugin and Ashlin, was opened on the Fair Day in 1866. It has windows by Micheál Healy and by Harry Clarke. The tower can be seen from a long way up the valley standing, as it does, on the high ground above the river. Zion Church in Rathgar and Rathfarnham Church both occupy similar exalted positions.

Donnybrook Church overlooks a granite obelisk, surrounded by cotoneaster on its little green island in the middle of a permanent traffic jam. It is worth braving the perils of the assembled cars and buses to read with reverence the inscription:

MDCCCXXXVIII

Erected to the memory of the late Alderman Arthur Morrison.
As Lord Mayor of the City of Dublin he was respected and esteemed
He was a sincere friend, charitable, kind, generous
As a Christian and citizen there were few to equal, none to surpass him.

Which leaves no doubt that he was an entirely admirable person — but does anybody know what, if anything, he did to deserve the honour of an obelisk?

At Anglesey Bridge the Dodder itself retires for a while behind houses and then runs between playing fields of various kinds. The bridge has been brutally treated by the building of walls and dumping of rubble. Its downstream face in particular is worth leaning over a wall to look at: a stately arch flanked with pyramid-shaped abutments, quite similar to those at Old Bawn. Back lanes off Anglesea Road (incorrectly spelt by the authorities and even by the luminaries of the Royal Dublin Society) give glimpses of the river but the easiest and most delightful approach to this stretch is through Herbert Park.

Herbert Park

The beautiful gardens, old shady trees and a bandstand belong to a long-past age of starched nurse-maids and well-dressed infants out for fresh air. But the attractions of parks and ducks last longer than that: nurse-maids and prams have been replaced by free-range children and bejeaned baby-minders and mums, even by male parents who would not have been seen in a more gracious age.

I have written much elsewhere about Herbert Park and could write more but the best description is the work of Dr Christy Boylan who prepared a descriptive leaflet which I quote in full. Dr Boylan's position in the Parks Department of the Corporation enables him to oversee the loving care which the gardeners and custodians lavish on one of the finest of many outstanding gardens in Dublin.

> The land was owned by the Earl of Pembroke who in 1903 offered the site (now comprising 32 acres) to the Pembroke Urban District Council for a public park. It was also considered by a committee for the Exhibition and this gave impetus to its development. The Exhibition was opened from May 4th to November 9th 1907 and was a great success. This exhibition was mooted at the turn of the century to help the economy of this country and to boost the cultural status and international standing of the ascendancy classes resident here at the time.

The original site was 53 acres and included portions of Aranmore, Argyle and St. Brendan's Roads. The main entrance gate to the exhibition was situated nearly opposite present day McCluskey Pub on Donnybrook Road. Massive exhibition stands were erected over a five year period and great trouble was taken to include exact replicas from countries from which original exhibits had been promised. For example, the site presently occupied by the Gaelic football pitch was given entirely to an Indian village. All the countries of the British Empire were represented and some very large buildings were constructed including a Central Palace with four wings to represent each province. All the buildings were removed afterwards and the only resemblance of the Exhibition today are the pond, pergola and some shelters.

Work then commenced on the design and layout of the Park and it was opened officially on the 19th August 1911 and named Herbert Park after the Right Hon. Sydney Herbert (1810-61), Lord Herbert of Lea, a former owner of the Fitzwilliam Estate and father of the Earl of Pembroke. Dublin Corporation acquired the Park in 1932 when the Pembroke and Rathmines Urban Councils were amalgamated with the city by an Act of Parliament.

The pergola at Herbert Park

Being located adjacent to the River Dodder, Herbert Park forms part of a linear park network being developed between the city and county along the banks of the River Dodder. Other parks along the Dodder include Dartry Park, Orwell Park and Bushy Park. It should also be noted that near the pond there once stood a house where lived a Mr. Ball, the gentleman whose name is given to the bridge crossing the River Dodder and known as Ballsbridge. When the pond was constructed it was part of a Canadian water shute which cost approximately £3,000 but it was a very popular feature as is indicated by receipts of £7,000 obtained during the period of the Exhibition.

In 1978 Dublin Corporation in conjunction with the Fisheries Board introduced a carp fish stock to the ponds in Herbert Park. This innovation has proved highly successful and there is now an excellent carp fish stock in the park and many other parks around the country have subsequently followed the initiative.

Sunken paths lead from open parkland to the upper pond area, generating an air of expectancy as the first glimpse of water unfolds. The upper island has been planted with Rhododendrons, Heathers and other ericaceous plants. The first to flower in February is Rhododendron Praecox, followed by Rhododendron Christmas Cheer and many others, producing lovely patches of colour to the end of June.

The facilities for active recreation in the park include 18 tennis courts, 3 football pitches, a bowling green, a croquet lawn and children's play area. The bowling green was developed in 1948 when the sport was at the peak of its popularity. Whilst many value these facilities, there is an even greater demand for the more passive use of Herbert Park and visitors have easy access of 10 entrances. A special feature is the Italian style pergola in the vicinity of which grow a wide range of plant material not found in parks in other parts of the city. These include alpine plants in the rockery, herbaceous plants forming a border and an array of climbing plants on the pergola. In 1988 a new dome was erected in the centre of the pergola replacing the original dome. In addition there is a display of seasonal bedding schemes adjacent to the major road named Herbert Park, which divides the park into two sections.

Many people enjoy taking a stroll in Herbert Park and perhaps sitting on a seat and enjoying the environment of mature trees and shrubs. Generally people visit neighbourhood parks from a distance of half a mile. But a 1980 study revealed that visitors to Herbert Park travel a longer distance because of the peace and quietness, extensive planting and wildlife.

There are many important trees in Herbert Park but perhaps the most famous were the double row of Wheatly Elms (Ulmus wheatleyi), planted by dignitaries between 1912-1916. These large majestic trees were a landmark in Dublin for many years but unfortunately they died, having been infected with Dutch Elm Disease and had to be removed. They have since been replaced by Hornbeam (Carpinus betulus fastigiata). These trees were planted to commemorate Ireland's first National Tree Week in 1985. A ceremonial planting was held with the Deputy Lord Mayor on Tuesday, March 12th 1985 and was attended by representative bodies of the Tree Council of Ireland.

Other trees in Herbert Park include Tilia platyphillos corallina (Lime), Beech (Fagus sylvatica) and Birch (Betula) and these include specimens of Acer platanoides (Norway Maple) which was planted on 11th November 1977 by Mrs L. Carter, mother of Mr Jimmy Carter, the then President of the United States. There is also a specimen of the Tree of Heaven, Ailanthus altissima planted by the President of the Asian Society, New York, to mark the Society's first visit to the Chester Beatty Library and Ireland. Another popular attraction in Herbert Park are the summer band performances and while a bandstand is situated in the open part of the Park, it is not as popular as the shelter near the pool because of more satisfactory acoustics.

Near the football pitches there are old cottages named after St Broc — a holy woman who at the time of the introduction of Christianity founded a church in the neighbourhood known as Domhnach-Broc, Church of St Broc, later to become Donnybrook.

Over the years, Herbert Park has matured and now provides a very restful and welcome oasis from the hustle and bustle of the city. It also provides a wide range of facilities required by the present generation, capable of being enjoyed by all.

The introduction of the carp was arranged by Jimmy Keaveny when he was Superintendent of the park. After 22 years some of the original stocking were still there in 1990, splendid fish of 12 pounds and more. They have survived in spite of such problems as a nefarious restaurateur who offered certain gurriers fabulous rewards for their capture. In good summers the carp are able to breed in Herbert Park but they are generally rare fish in Ireland because the water seldom gets warm enough.

Since 1989 tufted duck, the black drake with a big white patch on each flank, have lived in the pond together with the long-established mallard, moorhen and coot. Tufted duck came to dwell in the inner city parks of Dublin in the 1970s, a dramatic change of habits. Previously they would sometimes spend some weeks in the ponds in winter but there was no question of their staying permanently and breeding as they do now in Stephen's Green and the City Basin. The pioneers which came to Herbert Park in 1989 were drakes but it is likely that they will be followed by females and in due course rear families of little black ducklings.

Ballsbridge

Along the railings between park and river, a tarmac path runs at a high level. Steps at the northern end lead to a path just above the water. On the right bank gardens go down to the riverside and the houses behind them are screened by something of a jungle of escaped bushes. The line of jungle and gardens

Tufted duck

is broken for a little by the lawns of Merrion Cricket ground which go to the edge of the river, above a steep bank of glacial till. The left bank is very rigidly confined by concrete retaining walls, but willows have been planted on the level bits.

From time to time oystercatchers visit the cricket ground, black and white birds with long strong red bills. They do not catch a great many oysters there — nor do they find many between the tides in Dublin Bay where most of them forage. Cockles are the favourite food of oystercatchers by the seaside. In the Dodder valley they go as far inland as the lawns at Classon's Bridge and probably visit the other green spaces in the valley from time to time. Why they do this is something of a mystery. Dublin Bay offers plenty of suitable food and that is where these handsome black-and-white birds assemble by the thousand, coming inland only in twos and threes as a rule. Perhaps these are individualists who want to escape from the common herd and will accept earthworms instead of molluscs to satisfy their craving for originality.

Downstream of Herbert Park the Dodder flows between two of the major institutions of Dublin, one recently deceased, the other very much alive. On the left bank the great red bakery of Johnston, Mooney and O'Brien stands empty and unloved since 1989 — save by some property speculator. Opposite are the showgrounds of the Royal Dublin Society. The saddest thing about the demise of Johnston Mooney is that spectators at the Horse Show can no longer inhale the ambrosial vapours of fresh-baked bread which wafted across the river in days gone by.

The tail race from McGuirk's Mill passed underneath Donnybrook Road and ran parallel to the Dodder, close to the present day railings of Herbert Park. One remnant of a sluice, which controlled the water level at the mill, can still be seen. In the 19th century the site was occupied by Duffy and Son's calico print works which employed as many as 500 workers. Duffy and Son were taken over and closed down by a rival Manchester firm. Herbert Park occupies the site of the old drying green and the bakery grew up in the grounds of the factory.

A little group of mature poplars leans slightly towards the Dodder and away from the shade of the bakery. The downstream part of Johnston Mooney's is a fine Victorian structure, of red brick on top of a lower course of granite. Before bulk handling of grain and flour developed, a crane operated to lift sacks into the works. Its little roof still protrudes from the building and an opening three storeys high has been bricked in. Whatever development takes place on the site in future, the walk between river and property has been secured for the public under planning regulations.

The RDS

Opposite Johnston Mooney's, the show grounds of the Royal Dublin Society extend eastwards for nearly half a mile. The vista presented here by their side view is impressive when judged by the usual standards of the outsides of sporting arenas. The walls, of granite rather than concrete, help a lot and in spring the roadside is bright with the pink blossom of almond trees.

Ballsbridge and the RDS almost seem synonymous but in fact the connection has existed for less than half the Society's long life. In November 1877 its Council

announced that the Society had acquired an interest in 'a large field in the neighbourhood of Ball's Bridge'. In 1879, fifteen acres were leased from the Earl of Pembroke. George Wilkinson, the architect of Harcourt Street Station thirty years before, was commissioned to design the buildings. They were completed in 1881 and the first Ballsbridge Spring Show was held on 19-22 April. The Horse Show took place later the same year, a successor, if more genteel, to the abandoned fair of Donnybrook. The permanent buildings of the showgrounds were completed in 1883.

The Dodder invaded the RDS on 25th and 26th August 1986. The showgrounds formed a temporary lake with water one metre deep. Books on the lower shelves of the Society's library were flooded and a major rescue operation took place. The Dun Emer carpet woven within the Dodder valley in Dundrum in 1935 for the RDS Council Room was also a temporary victim of the flood. In this case the enforced cleaning and restoration brought back brilliant colours which most people had forgotten.

The showgrounds, with their immaculately cropped grass and lovely flower beds, scarcely seem part of the wilderness. But wild nature is not so easily displaced. The grandstand enclosure for many years has provided a safe retreat for a family of foxes.

A corner of the grounds between the river and the RDS were Township property before the Society acquired its land. Pembroke Town Hall was built there but became redundant when Rathmines and Pembroke lost their independence in 1930. It now serves as the headquarters of the Vocational Education Committee. A public library has also been built on the site and, between river and road, a public loo. The latter amenity in red brick has no special architectural merit but the planners were clearly proud of their contribution to the comfort of the citizens. So they emblazoned the date 1943 on a plaque of granite between the entrances for Ladies and Gentlemen.

A low weir crosses the river here and marks the limit reached by high tides, the sea nowadays lying a little less than 2 km downstream. Various public authorities have been engaged for many centuries in pushing the sea away from Ballsbridge. The geological map marks an area of 'alluvium', sand carried down by the river and spread out in the shape of a fan. It extends from the seashore back as far as the Beaver Row waterfall. The Dodder flowed freely through this delta, changing path from time to time after its highest floods, until the 17th century.

Then began the succession of harbour works on the Liffey which continues to this day and which naturally impinged on the Dodder. The works transformed the Dodder from a river in its own right to being a tributary — since they extended the Liffey past the Dodder mouth into Dublin Bay at Poolbeg. By 1728 the Dodder, marked as 'Donny Brook R.' on de Gomme's New and Correct Map of that date, was confined to a narrow course between great expanses of reclaimed land.

A house owned by a Mr Ball stood in the vicinity at the beginning of the 17th century but no bridge was to be built until 1751 — the river would have been fordable at least at low tide before the days of its construction. Who Mr Ball was, or whether his descendants were still living in the district, nobody knows. But his name was firmly attached to the bridge when it was built.

By the standards of Dodder crossings the first one enjoyed a long life, no less than forty years before rebuilding was necessary in 1791. The next major repairs took place in 1835 and the final work, in 1904, was a combination of repairs and widening. This was a great success and resulted in a very pleasing structure in pale grey limestone. Mr Ball lost his apostrophe a long time ago: the map of 1814 writes 'Balls Bridge' as does that of 1937. But the modern maps have abandoned even the decency of two separate words.

Meeting the tide

The left bank of the Dodder immediately downstream of Ballsbridge vies with the tannery at Oldbawn and the papermills at Clonskeagh in competing for the prize for the least prepossessing aspect. It may even be considered the winner since it would be possible to screen the factory and attempts have been made to hide the tannery with cypress trees. But the intransigent walls of bank, one-time laundry and garage almost defy adornment: window boxes and creeper, perhaps?

The little roadway, Beatty's Avenue, on the right bank is more attractive and boasts one of the very few riverside restaurants on the Dodder. This actually faces the river in contrast to the majority of the pubs which firmly turn their backs on it. The point is marked on the map as the highest to which medium tides flow and the river is crossed by an aqueduct carrying water from the Vartry, as well as from the Dodder, to the city. The iron pipe is supported by two piers: one an original entirely of cut granite, the other partly repaired in concrete.

The cottages on the right have developed in their day from labourers' dwellings to bijou town houses. The hedges in the little gardens are usually seething with sparrows, supposedly common birds but in fact very strictly confined to particular habitats. You can walk for miles of Dodderside, admiring herons, dippers, kingfishers and grey wagtails but without a single sparrow. Beatty's Avenue offers all these species and more. In Dublin the privet hedge seems to be almost an essential to support a sparrow population.

The river bed begins to show signs of the action of the tide and presents mud banks exposed at low water. The highest of the banks have wild flowers in profusion: balsam thrives there, together with butterbur, willow herb and reeds. The forlorn look of the riverside brightens a little after passing beneath the railway bridge where the playing fields of Marian College provide a certain amount of open space and mature trees: limes, beeches and horse

chestnuts. Sycamores have a precarious foothold in the spaces between the stones of the wall above the river.

The last of the mills

On the left bank, where the gardens of the newer houses of Lansdowne Road go down to the river, the lowest mill on the Dodder stood. It was fed by the tailrace from Duffy and Son's at Ballsbridge. This was Bourke's flour mill. Robert Mallet wrote at the end of his section on the mills:

> We have thus traced the course of every branch of the river Dodder, from its sources to its mouth, and stated the general features of its line, and of the power existing upon it.
>
> The total occupied fall upon all branches of the river is 370 feet 4¾ inches, of which 87 feet one inch exist on the natural channel of the river, between Diana and Templeogue; 181 feet 10 inches on the artificial channel, between Templeogue and the Liffey; and 101 feet 5¾ inches upon the natural channel between Templeogue and the Liffey at Ringsend.
>
> On comparing these with the longitudinal section of the river, so far as same is had from the Ordnance Survey Levels, combined with those taken for this report, and which are forwarded herewith, it will be seen how large a portion of the total fall has been wasted by the mal-position of the mills.

Brilliant engineer though he was, Mallet could not have foreseen in 1844 how quickly steam would replace the need for waterwheels, nor how the mills would one by one fall into disuse and decay.

There was one more weir on the Dodder, close to Lansdowne Road stadium, immediately downstream of New Bridge. This was part of the works of Haigh's distillery which occupied the ground to the east of the present Herbert Road. Too close to the tide to provide power, the weir made a pond to maintain a supply of cooling water. New Bridge sadly lacks a name plate, but its three-arch

A lamp on Ballsbridge.

design is very similar to that of the nearby London Bridge and it probably dates to the 1850s. There are delightful little triangles of park on both sides of New Bridge with shrubs and seats where you can relax and watch the river go by with its seagulls and mallard.

Grey mullet come in shoals to this part of the river in spring and stay till autumn. Although breeding and spending most of their lives in the sea, they can accept fresh water and live happily in tidal rivers. Mullet leave the estuaries and move offshore for the winter. Big fish, the same size as summer salmon, they swim here and there lazily, near the surface as a rule. But sometimes the shoal develops a fit of frenzied activity and they leap about, often breaking the surface. Very good to eat, they are quite difficult to catch since they feed largely on plankton and have no time for enticing worms or lures. However, urban mullet can learn to eat many unlikely things including breadcrumbs.

The reclaimed land

New Bridge crosses the Dodder where it takes a sharp turn to the left, its last kick of freedom before the engineers of the 18th century encased it within straight walls all the way to the sea. The great and glorious rugby football ground of Lansdowne Road occupies the left bank here and, a little further down, the playing fields of Londonbridge Road are on the right. Shelbourne Road greyhound stadium lies still further down, on the left. All of these spaces for what the Planners term 'active recreation' take advantage of the level ground provided by reclaimed land behind the sea walls. Besides the vigorous humanity found in these parts, black-headed gulls and oystercatchers gather to hunt for worms when the combination of rain and athletes makes the ground soft.

A pleasant footpath, spread with gravel, leads down the left bank as far as London Bridge. Hawthorns and willows and other trees have been planted there recently, and there are occasional self-seeded sycamores. Alexanders cover much of the ground together with magnificent tangles of blackberries on the river bank. At low tide in winter redshanks feed on the mud banks, wading birds with long red legs and beaks. The left bank slopes to the river's edge;

the right has been built up with limestone blocks invaded by sycamores and alders.

London Bridge was built of timber and, after the usual vicissitudes, replaced in stone in 1857. Very low and very flat it has three round arches. Downstream, the influence of fresh water is greatly reduced and seaweed appears, festooning stones and pieces of wood, anything which gives it a firm anchorage. The brown species is bladder wrack, its fronds bearing air bladders which buoy them up and keep them close to the surface when the tide rises.

On the level ground on the left bank, parallel to South Lotts Road, a 'rope walk' is marked on Taylor's map of Dublin in the early 19th century. Part of the site is occupied now by the greyhound track and part by houses. In rope making men and horses walked in a straight line first laying and then twisting the strands. The walk extended from Bath Avenue to Ringsend Road, about a quarter of a mile.

Herring gull and great black-backed gull join the black-headed gulls which are plentiful along most of the length of the Dodder. Cormorants keep to the deeper part of the estuary: since they are quite big birds and hunt by swimming under water they cannot live in the shallows. In summer terns, graceful white birds with black caps and swallow-tails, flit about, diving to the surface to snatch silvery fish. They nest nearby on the platform around an island lighthouse in the Liffey.

Houses and gardens reach to the river's edge on the left bank downstream of London Bridge preventing direct access. A little farther down there are rowing clubs and boat slips. A footpath runs along an embankment by the right bank, passing a complex of buildings, some in neat limestone masonry, others of red brick with a tall chimney. They are all parts of a pumping station, built in 1881 to raise sewage from the low-lying reclaimed land up to the level of the treatment plant at Ringsend. Steam pumps, tragically scrapped in 1953, were replaced by electric pumps with a diesel standby. In the 1980s, a little over a hundred years after the station was built, the sewage was directed to the new main tunnel so that pumping is needed only when storms overload the system.

Below the level of the footpath, downstream of the

pumping station, there are pretty terraces of brightly painted one-storey houses, all built on the reclaimed land. Then the ground rises to the older dwellings and shops of Ringsend. Before the sea walls were built early in the 18th century, Ringsend and Irishtown stood above the level of the tides, occupying a sand spit along the margin of Dublin Bay. They were isolated communities, approachable on land only from the direction of Sandymount.

Ringsend and its bridges

Ringsend Bridge, the most elegant of many fine crossings, had the most chequered career of all. Gerard Boate in 1643 begins the story in his account of the Dodder saying, with reference to the drowning of Mr John Usher:

> Since that time a stone bridge hath been built over that brook (as over Drumconran-water there hath been one from antient times) upon the way betwixt Dublin and Rings-end; which was hardly well accomplished, when the brook in one of those furious risings quite altered its channel for a good way, so as it did not pass under the Bridge as before, but just before the foot of it, letting the same stand upon dry land, and consequently making it altogether useless: in which perverse course it continued, until per force it was constrained to return to its old channel, and to keep within the same.

Before long, in spite of the said constraint, the Dodder duly destroyed the bridge described by Boate. It was replaced in 1727 and survived till 1782, but the next, built in 1789 stood for only three years. Michael Barry in 'Across Deep Waters' takes up the story:

> The present bridge, with solid abutments, was built as a replacement in 1803. This granite bridge incorporated many contemporary advances in bridge construction. The single arch is of flat elliptical shape, allowing the roadway and parapet to have lines which are nearly horizontal. The curve of the arch continues downwards to form a paved river bed, or inverted arch.

An interesting detail here is the use of *Cornes de Vache*. This chamfering of the edge of the arch can be seen rising up from the springing stone. This streamlines the bridge to some degree against the rigours of flooding.

Writing in 1952 Maurice Craig mentioned that Ringsend Bridge was threatened with demolition. Thirty-nine years later it still stands in all its beauty. Neither the Dodder nor official vandalism have prevailed.

The right bank downstream of Ringsend Bridge is occupied by blocks of Corporation flats built of yellow brick. The left bank has stone steps leading to a quay, long since abandoned by shipping and in 1989 inhabited by mobile homes sheltered by the walls of decaying warehouses and cottages. Across the river is the last of the Dodder-side churches, St Patrick's. It probably doesn't think of itself as a church by a river and, in common with so many other Irish buildings, stands with its back to the water. At the time it was built, the odours of the Dodder would have offered something less than sanctity.

The last dwelling on the Dodder, the harbourmaster's house is surrounded by an impregnable wall above which a solitary sycamore looks out, bearing in its branches a magpie nest. Around the corner lie the three great locks of the Grand Canal Dock. The biggest, Camden Lock, built in 1790 and still in excellent repair, is capable of admitting quite large vessels to the dock. The next two, Buckingham and Westmoreland, were both built six years later. Buckingham Lock has fallen on evil days and its seaward gates are gaunt wooden skeletons. But they do provide a foothold for a Dodder kingfisher who perches there eyeing the mingled waters of Dodder, Liffey and Grand Canal.

Shops and factories and homes of Ringsend, including some of the finest modern Inner City developments, occupy the right bank where Thorncastle Street leads down to the Liffey side. St Patrick's Rowing Club has a boathouse on the Liffey Quay while Premier Byproducts occupy the bank of the Dodder and an old boatslip enters the water beside it.

Ringsend is part of the Liffey rather than the Dodder and anyway deserves a history to itself. Until the 17th century it was a port in its own right and many boats landed there rather than proceeding up the Liffey to the city of Dublin. Oliver Cromwell, with 12,000 troops in 1649, was one of the less happily remembered visitors. The Dodder at the time formed an anchorage off the main channel.

Between 1707 and 1728 the Great South Wall was built as far downstream as the Dodder where Sir John Rogerson's Quay ends. The building of the South Wall was eventually completed with the Poolbeg Lighthouse in 1762. Behind the wall at first there was relatively little dry land and the sloblands were gradually reclaimed and built over.

And so to the Liffey

Thus was the wayward river finally tamed. For many years she has languished in an area of dockland and gasworks with their inevitable accompaniments of noise and smell. But she has come through worse. Disastrous floods, though not quite vanquished, seldom happen more often than twice in a hundred years. Industrial pollution from the old mills together with sewage from housing estates are almost completely under control. The extraction of water by the mills which left miles of the river bed dry and devoid of life has gone for ever.

Winds of change blow around the Dodder mouth, too. Natural gas has replaced the filth of the old works. Shipping has largely moved downstream of the East Link Bridge, new homes are appearing at Ringsend and across the Liffey the Point Theatre has transformed the old railway building. There are bright prospects for the area with its open spaces, free from traffic, on the quaysides and the calm water of the Grand Canal Dock. Some day it will be a colourful centre for canoes and sail boards, with seats and shady trees. Plans unveiled and work begun in 1990 will transform the mouth of the Dodder from wasteland to an area of affluence. Meanwhile the mullet splash, the seagulls clamour and the terns flit gently above the water.

Their ancestors lived there long before the days of Finn, before the very earliest Irish people came to gather shell-fish between the tides at the mouth of the Dodder. Now the Dodder has been transformed from an uncontrollable torrent to a mild river, flowing for much of its length between walls of stone or concrete. There are fewer wild creatures and they no long threaten us nor compete with us for scarce food. Greater stress in urban life together with more time for leisure gives the wilderness an ever-increasing value. Much has been saved in the valley of the Dodder.

Bridge inscription.

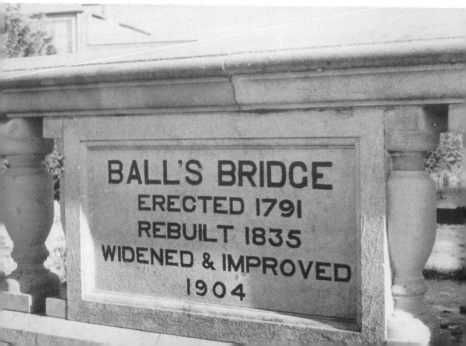

BALL'S BRIDGE
ERECTED 1791
REBUILT 1835
WIDENED & IMPROVED
1904

CHAPTER 6

Floods and flood control

The fury of the Dodder has yet to be brought under complete control. The greatest disaster took place as recently as 1986, the latest of a succession whose historical records go back to the 17th century. Gerard Boate writing in 1643 gives a general discussion on the smaller rivers of Ireland and their 'swelling and overflowing'. Then he takes the Tolka and Dodder as special examples, the Dodder as extra special:

> Of these dangerous Brooks there are two hard by Dublin, both running into the Haven somewhat more than a mile from the city, the one at the North-side thereof, a little below the Village Dromconran, which is seated upon the Highway from Dublin to Drogheda; and the other at the South-side, close by the Rings-end. This called Rafernam-water of the village by which it passeth two miles from the sea and the same distance from Dublin, is far the worst of the two, as taking its beginning out of those great mountains South-wards from Dublin, from whence after any great rain such abundance of water descending to it, that the same, which at other times is of very little depth, groweth thereby so deep, and exceeding violent, that many persons have lost their lives therein; amongst others Mr *John Usher*, Father to Sir *William Usher* that now is, who was carryed by the current, no body being able to succour him, although many persons, and of his neerest friends, both afoot and horseback were by on both the sides.

Boate goes on to describe the fate of the bridge at Ringsend, already quoted on page 151. He was fully aware of the importance of the mountains in contributing to the fury of the Dodder's floods. Since his time, many people concerned themselves with the river and various works were undertaken in attempts to control it.

Robert Mallet's plans

The *Report on the Dodder Reservoirs* by Robert Mallet was prepared in 1844 under the *Drainage and Improvement of Water-power, Act 5 & 6 Victoria, c 89*. His plan for reservoirs had two aims: firstly for providing a more reliable water supply for the mills and secondly for controlling the floods. The picture Mallet paints showed that little had happened to improve matters since the days of Gerard Boate, two centuries earlier:

> A few years only have elapsed since one of the frequent floods of the River Dodder occurred so suddenly, at night, of such magnitude, and attended with such appalling circumstances, of destruction to property and danger to human life, as to have aroused the public concern for the damage resulting; and which finally led to expensive litigation betwixt parties subjected thereto, and to the subsequent compulsory expenditure of large sums in the execution of works near the mouth of the river, only intended to ward off the destructive effects of future inundations, but not attempting to control them. Yet similar floods, though fortunately not to such a formidable extent, occur upon this river many times every year.

He goes on to explain why the Dodder's floods are so very serious, above all that the river is unusually short in comparison with the height of the greater part of its catchment area:

> The declivity is rapid upon every part of the river in proportion to its length, except for the last three and a half or four miles nearest its mouth; but the amount of fall is nowhere answerable to that which exists in the valley of its sources; and hence it is that all the conditions capable of producing destructive floods upon a river of such a magnitude are found conspiring here — a catchment large in proportion to the length of the river-course, the watershed, at first, unusually rapid; and the waters thus accumulated, rolled along channels subjected to many natural and artificial obstructions: and at length debouched, before reaching the sea, upon a plane of very trifling declivity, and

over which the waters are in danger of spreading in every flood.

The results of this state of unstable regimen on the river, are that its bed is in a continual state of change. An average width below Oldbawn of about 50 feet, would be amply sufficient for the discharge of its average waters; but a wide-spread strand, of unproductive shingle, covers its banks for miles in length at either side. In some places, as above Templeogue, at Ball's Bridge, &c., the bed is in progress of filling up by the recurrent deposit of gravel; while, in others, as below Templeogue, at and below Rathfarnham, &c., the bed has been lowered, or become excavated by the rush of water, aided, however, by the practice of carrying away shingle from the bed, at particular spots, for the purpose of road-making, &c., an evil which ought, in future, to be abated. If the excavation of gravel were carried on under proper supervision, and according to rule, benefit, rather than evil, would result to the river course. As things are, many of the weirs, retaining walls, and other structures have become undermined and in danger of destruction by the combined action of floods, and the indiscriminate carrying away of gravel from the bed.

Mallet reckoned that not less than 50 acres of land had been carried away in the preceding hundred years and that a total of 13 miles of bank were currently in danger of erosion. He referred to the spoiling of crops by periodical flooding, the removal of haystacks and the fact that much of the riverside land could be used only for pasture. Other parts were covered with shingle, gravel and sand of use only:

. . . for the precarious collection of the worst description of road material, by persons who, I am informed, pay nothing to the landed proprietors . . . .

Floods in the past

Particularly bad floods were recorded in 1787, 1794, 1802, 1807 and 1851. Accurate records of rainfall began to be collected in the 1880s when the Glenasmole reservoirs were being built. During the period when that work was in progress, two serious floods took place: one on 1st September 1883, the other on 16th October 1886. The first of these overflowed the unfinished dams and removed large chunks of the construction. But by the time the second came, the builders were ready and no serious damage resulted. The 24 hour rainfall on the first was 96 mm and on the second slightly less.

In the course of the 20th century, or at least of its first ninety years, the Dodder overflowed its banks seven times. I still have happy memories of the 1946 flood when, at the age of ten, I splashed through a great puddle along the edge of the road just upstream of Orwell Bridge where the retaining wall had been ripped away. At Rathfarnham Weir that day the water, instead of falling from a height into the pool below, rushed headlong in an unbroken brown mass, curving gently downwards where it swept over the waterfall.

However, the flood of 1946 was nothing compared with those which took place in 1905 and 1986, both on the same day, 25th August. The first was the highest ever recorded at Glenasmole where its flow was calculated to be between 99

Date stone on public loo at Ballsbridge.

and 119 cubic metres per second. One cubic metre of water weighs one ton, so in round figures 100 tons of water moved past every second. The energy involved is formidable and on that occasion was enough to carry away the bridge at Castlekelly.

In 1986 the flow at Orwell Bridge, 230 cubic metres per second, was greater than it had been in 1905. The 1986 flood at Castlekelly, however, was less than the earlier one. Apparently in 1905 the rain fell mainly in the mountains. In 1986 the downpour extended far and wide throughout the counties of Dublin and Wicklow so that the tributaries of the Dodder as well as its headwaters made their impact.

Hurricane Charlie — 1986

Pride of place therefore was yielded to the events associated with Hurricane Charlie. The 24-hour rainfall at Castlekelly was 190.2 mm, more than double the maximum for the 19th-century floods. The flow gauge at Orwell Bridge was quite unable to cope and disappeared beneath the flood so that its height could only be calculated from the level reached by the debris left after the waters subsided. The capacity of the flow gauge has duly been increased.

Date on Anglesey Bridge.

The damage is described by Jack M Keyes of Dublin Corporation in *The Engineer's Journal* for November 1987 and in greater detail in a paper in 1988 by P Hennigan, J McDaid and J Keyes. The situation had begun to look ominous at midday on 25th August 1986 when the weather forecast announced continuous heavy rain. The hope that the depression would head off across the Irish Sea towards Wales and that Dublin would escape prolonged rain was dashed at an early stage. Early in the evening the possibility of serious flooding was confirmed and by 6.00 pm the Lower Dodder Road at Orwell Bridge was impassable — just the same place where I had so happily paddled forty years before.

At 7.30 the situation was really serious. The whole surface drainage system became overloaded and the Dodder continued to rise inexorably. By 11.00 pm houses were flooded as far back as Dodder Park Road together with all the low-lying dwellings nearer the river. More roads became impassable and the attempts to staunch the floods with sandbags failed completely — all the effort then had to go to rescuing the marooned citizens. The flood reached its peak at 2.00 am the following morning and eight hours later the Dodder had returned to its proper channel.

The river left its channel at thirteen points in all, beginning at Lower Dodder Road. An estimated 25 cubic metres per second flowed down Anglesea Road and the water, far from confining itself to the low-lying banks of the river, rampaged through the gardens of Sandymount and other distant regions which had never even thought of themselves as lying in the valley of the Dodder. In all, four hundred 'properties' were flooded, flood being defined as an inundation of downstairs or basement floor area. Depths of up to 2.5 metres were recorded.

After the flood, the ground was coated with a 'mass of sticky, silty material over much of the flood plain'. Wooden floors were severely damaged and carpets and furniture ruined. Gullies and sewers and ditches were blocked, walls and trees knocked down.

Calculations, based on the recorded flows of the time and on older records, suggested that this was a one-in-two-thousand-year flood. The engineers who made this estimate found it hard to believe and pointed out that the data available to them were inadequate. They would prefer to go on the safe side and predict one such flood per hundred years. The problem with such statistics is that they do not necessarily mean that there is a period of grace of two thousand years or a century or whatever. The next flood could come next year without making liars of the statisticians.

In 1987 the cost of making good the damage to the river banks, the weirs and the parkland was estimated at £900,000. Insurance claims for property were in the order of £6 million and the cost of preventing the recurrence of such a disaster computed as £10 million.

This was found to be an underestimate and a figure of about £100 million has been mentioned. Floods of the size of Hurricane Charlie's are so rare that such expenditure could not be justified. This is good news to those who love the Dodder because it means that trees and weirs need not be destroyed by the drainage authorities.

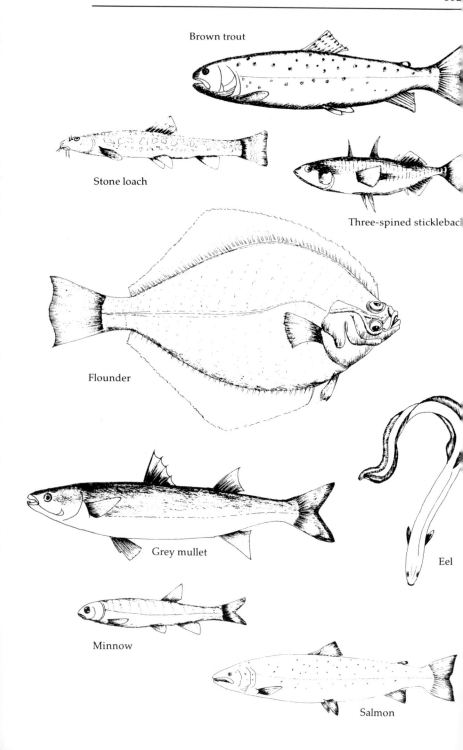

Brown trout

Stone loach

Three-spined stickleback

Flounder

Grey mullet

Eel

Minnow

Salmon

CHAPTER 7

Fishes and fishing

The restoration of the fish population of the Dodder is one of the minor triumphs of the 20th century. Long, long ago the building of the mill-dams confined salmon and sea trout to the lower reaches. It was not until 1925 that a law was made which required the builders of weirs to incorporate a fish pass. By that time all the Dodder weirs were well established and most of them continue to this day to block the upstream journeys of trout and salmon.

Between Firhouse and Rathfarnham, the Dodder dried out in the days of the watermills. Meanwhile the paper-mills and tanneries and maybe even the calico printing works all discharged their waste directly to the river. So did the houses. However, fish did survive in the upper reaches.

The fishes

William Handcock, writing in the 1870s, not only told the first fish stories of the Dodder but personally added to its fauna:

> The Sheep-hole . . . abounds with fine trout, which are fished for most assiduously all the season by Dubliners. The trout are so experienced, that they know every fly or artificial bait in Martin Kelly's, and are not to be taken by fair means. Sometimes the natives put in quick-lime when the river is low, and thus kill numbers. It is soon refilled, for the upper waters above Castle Kelly are preserved, and abound with small trout. The other kinds of fish in this river are eels, sticklebacks, locheen or gudgeon, and minnows. The last were not known in the river until about twenty years ago, when we brought a number from Lough Dan to our ponds, from whence they spread into the river, and are now to be found in myriads.

Trout and salmon

Brown trout continue to thrive in the waters above Castlekelly. They need clean water flowing over a bed of gravel to spawn in and there is no shortage of that in the three tributaries. Early in the new year the trout scoop out hollows in the gravel in which they lay their eggs: big eggs by the normal standards of fish, the size of petits pois but with a beautiful orange colour. A one-pound trout produces about 500 eggs each season. After they are laid the female completes the nest by covering the eggs with gravel. The nest is called a 'redd' and neither parent pays any further attention to their offspring — other than eating them on occasion.

The eggs hatch in spring and the trout from the 'fry' stage onwards will be fiercely territorial: each tries to establish its own area of stream bed and chases all neighbours and relatives out of sight. Most of them die as a result, many being eaten by herons and kingfishers, others simply starving and disappearing. The survivors move downstream as they grow bigger and the upper lake provides a generous living space with plenty of food. The exclusion of the acid water off the moorland from the upper lake adds to its attractions for the trout.

The water which the 19th-century planners needed for the domestic supply is relatively rich in lime and also in nitrogen. Because of this, the insects and other food organisms which the trout need are plentiful. The more acidic, upstream reaches, however, are very good for the younger trout. On the one hand they produce enough food for small fish and on the other they are too poor for the big ones which, if they stayed around, would certainly eat many of the young. Trout are no respecters of the right to life of their tender offspring.

Between the lower lake and Fort Bridge there is more spawning space and nursery ground for the young trout. But from that waterfall all the way downstream, the Dodder is not an ideal habitat for breeding trout. The old mill dams and weirs have created a succession of pools where the water flows over a bed of large stones or of silt with relatively little gravel. So there is not much room for spawning and the great majority of wild trout in these reaches have dropped downstream from Castlekelly. Because of the waterfalls, few of them are ever able to make their way back to the spawning grounds.

Every year some sea trout are seen in the lower reaches of the Dodder. They are rather strange creatures whose exact life history has yet to be worked out. Brown trout are the lake or river fish which spend all their lives in fresh water. Sea trout, or white trout, behave like salmon. At one or two years old they turn a silvery colour and swim down to the sea. There they stay for at least a few months and often for a year or more. They feed and grow quickly, then come back to spawn. This much is known for certain.

The mystery is whether all the young of a pair of sea trout will themselves go to sea or whether some will turn into brown trout and stay in the river. It is certain that when two brown trout spawn, some of their offspring may change into sea trout. Whatever the truth may be, the fact remains that the Dodder has far fewer sea trout than do most rivers of its size. The cause lies again in the multiplicity of mill-dams which prevent spawning in the lower reaches.

Salmon in the Dodder are even rarer than sea trout. In 1989 two were actually caught and six or seven could be seen below Beaver Row weir. After Hurricane Charlie some succeeded in swimming over the flooded weirs and going as far upstream as Templeogue. Salmon breed in winter in much the same manner as trout. But they have to go to sea at an age of one or two years. Most of them stay away for a little more than one year and return in summer as 'grilse', weighing on average about 2 kg. The bigger salmon have spent longer in the sea, usually two years, occasionally more. The reason that salmon are so rare in the Dodder is that they are never able to spawn there because the weirs keep them far away from the gravel beds that they need. Nearly all salmon return to spawn in the river they were born in. Therefore Liffey salmon head back up the Liffey. Those that turn away from it and go into the Dodder have lost their way.

Eels and others

Far and away the most remarkable fish in the Dodder is the eel. Eels travel at least as far upstream as Firhouse Weir

Township boundary mark

The remarkable thing is that they never breed in the Dodder — nor anywhere else in Europe. All European eels spawn in the Sargasso Sea, drift across the Atlantic and, as very small 'elvers', swim into rivers in spring. The elvers, little needle-like creatures 6 or 7 cm long, can actually leave the water and climb up damp mosses by the edges of waterfalls. That is how they come to inhabit such places as the Rathfarnham stretches of the Dodder.

Eels generally feed at night time, using their incredibly acute sense of smell to locate insect larvae and other small creatures. However, they enjoy warmth and from time to time on bright days come into the open to lie almost motionless and sunbathe. In autumn they burrow into the mud and sleep the winter away, coming out again to lead an active life in April. Eels breed once in a lifetime. They prepare for spawning when they are big enough and old enough, in Ireland at least six years old but usually more, between ten and fifteen. At this stage they stop feeding and in autumn when the weather is wet and the river flooded the eels head back to the ocean. Almost miraculously they navigate across more than a thousand miles to find the Sargasso Sea once more. Nobody, by the way, has ever seen a breeding eel out there. But there are millions and millions of very small baby ones which goes to show that the adults *must* be able to do it.

Two species of fish in the Dodder go under the name of *pinkeen*: the stickleback and the minnow. The term *pinkeen* is a very interesting one. It is accepted as of English origin, but the English word is no longer used and does not appear in the best dictionaries. In the 17th century, when the first minnows were brought to Ireland, they had an alternative name of *penk*. It seems that *penk* then acquired the Irish diminutive *-ín*. Anyway, small stream fish are pinkeens even to Dubliners with a minimal knowledge of Irish or Elizabethan English.

The stickleback is a native species, found in all parts of the country and sharing with trout and eel the ability to live in salt or fresh water. This ability is an essential feature of a native Irish freshwater fish. As long ago as the 12th century Giraldus Cambrensis, who made a list of the fish species in Irish rivers and lakes, pointed this out. No others could make their way to the island of Ireland.

Stickleback are aggressive fish which, like the trout, establish territories and chase away others of their own kind. Therefore you never catch more than a few stickleback in one place. Of the few one is likely to be a male, distinguished in the breeding season by brilliant pinkish red colouring; any others will be female. The male builds a barrel-shaped nest of pieces of weed and entices his chosen females to lay their eggs inside it. He then adopts all the responsibilities of parenthood, carefully guarding the nest and, in due course, the young.

Minnows, in contrast, live in large, sometimes enormous, shoals with hundreds or even thousands of individuals. They breed in summer, letting their eggs fall on the gravel and abandoning them. In winter the shoals break up and the individual minnow retire to deep water or shelter under stones. Floods are likely to be fatal to the majority of the minnow population, exept where they are able to find sheltered waters or deep mill ponds. Because of their large numbers and habit of swimming near the surface in bright water where they are easy to see, minnow are probably the staple diet of the Dodder's kingfishers.

One more species of fish is found in the Dodder above the tide, the loach or stone-loach or *collacrue*, a brown speckled fish about the shape and size of a pencil stub. *Collacrue* is derived from the Irish *cailleach rua*, red hag. They are not particularly red, but the hag part of the name refers to the three whisker-like pairs of barbels around the mouth. The loach feeds at night, finding its prey animals with the aid of the very sensitive barbels. Like the minnow, they breed in early summer, laying eggs amongst the gravel.

One of the most interesting things about the fish life of the dodder is its racial purity. Salmon, trout, eel and stickleback are all native species, only minnow and loach are exotics. Most Irish lowland rivers now hold large stocks of introduced fish. Pike and perch arrived in the 17th century. Rudd came later but nobody knows just when. Finally, beginning in the 1960s, roach were spread around the country, on purpose in some cases, by accident in others. All of these species compete with trout which, quite apart from being a native species worthy of preservation, are better for eating than any of the introduced ones.

Because of their difficulties in competing with the other
species, trout are rare in the lowland reaches of most of the
rivers of Europe. Big trout in rivers such as the Dodder,
although commonplace in Ireland, are an almost unique
feature of our wildlife.

In the tidal part of the river, downstream of Ballsbridge,
mullet come in the shoals already mentioned (page 149).
They are summer visitors, retiring to the sea and generally
moving south in the winter. Mullet are warm water fish,
their nearest breeding place being on the south coast.

One other species probably lives in the Dodder, though
I have yet to see one. This is the flounder or 'fluke', a flat
fish which breeds in deepish water offshore in the sea.
Small ones, a few centimetres long, swim into river
estuaries and may stay and grow there for a year or two
before returning to the sea to spawn. Provided there are no
waterfalls, flounder swim into fresh water. Their brown
colour, marked with a scattering of orange spots or
blotches, keeps them perfectly camouflaged on muddy or
stony bottoms.

The least known of the fishes of the Dodder is one of the
most remarkable, a sort of 'living fossil' whose ancestry
goes back far beyond that of the 'modern' species. It is the
brook lamprey and looks rather like a small eel. But its skin
is marked with a pattern of spots and, much more important, the lamprey has no jaws, in fact no bones at all. Its
mouth is a circular opening and can hold on to stones by
suction.

The brook lampreys usually keep out of sight, except in
summer when they mate and make hollows to lay their
eggs in by moving the smaller stones in gravelly parts of
the river. The eggs hatch into larvae which resemble
earthworms rather than fish. The larvae live for as much as
four years in the mud where they feed on dead plant and
animal material. Then they develop into the form of the
adult which has nothing to do in life but mate and lay eggs.
Adult brook lampreys eat nothing and do not live long after
spawning. Other species of lamprey grow much bigger, go
to sea and feed parasitically on living fish.

Ringsend Church

Water quality

Trout and eel live at opposite extremes of the degree of need for clean water. Trout lead very active lives, always swimming gently against the current, waiting to snap up any passing food animal and often dashing about to chase away their neighbours. This endless activity requires an abundant supply of dissolved oxygen in the water. Eels on the other hand can rest on the bottom or burrow into the mud to remain motionless for hours or even days at a time and to sleep all through the winter. Their oxygen requirements at such times are very low. However, even eels need plenty of oxygen when they are active and feeding.

The water in the upper reaches of the Dodder is saturated with oxygen, dissolved from the pure mountain air as the stream splashes over the stones and rushes down the waterfalls. This is the ideal habitat of trout. In the lower reaches, where the water flows more slowly, much of the oxygen is supplied by the submerged plants: by the higher plants such as water cress, by the submerged mosses and green slime and by the microscopic algae of the plankton which float freely in the water. The plankton are most plentiful in the lakes where there is no current to carry them away.

Nearly all the plants provide a surplus of oxygen. On rare occasions in the Dodder they can be too much of a good thing. Plants, like animals, have to respire: to take in oxygen and release carbon dioxide. Photosynthesis, the process which gives off oxygen, takes place only in the daytime, while respiration goes on day and night. If there are too many plants, the flow of water is too slow and the temperature too high. So much oxygen is used up at night by the plants that fish, especially trout, are killed. This has seldom, if ever, happened in the Dodder.

But the oxygen can be removed in other ways, all of them associated with the doings of the human population. When organic waste, waste material derived from plants or animals, goes into the water it is attacked by bacteria which ultimately transform it to carbon dioxide and water. But the process which brings this about needs oxygen and therefore organic waste in a river uses up the oxygen. This has caused very serious trouble in the Dodder in the past, indeed in the 19th century few fish were able to live in the reaches downstream of Bohernabreena.

With the demise of the papermills, tanneries and other factories which discharged huge quantities of organic waste into the river, the situation improved dramatically. There were still some problem areas in the 1960s but the combined efforts of the workers of the Dublin Board of Fishery Conservators (now the Dublin Regional Fisheries Board) and the members of the Dodder Anglers' Club brought the perpetrators to justice and industrial pollution nowadays is as near as can be to a memory of the bad old days. Even so, accidents will happen and a spillage of diesel oil in the Jobstown River caused a fish kill in the Dodder near Firhouse in 1990.

The remaining source of pollution is the particularly unpleasant one of domestic sewage. Effluents reach the Dodder from the direction of Tallaght at a point between Old Bawn Bridge and Firhouse Weir, from the affluent suburbs of Terenure and Kimmage through Bushy Park and from many sources along the Dundrum Stream discharging near Milltown. These together consitute a difficult problem because the owners of the dwellings are probably unaware of what they are doing and the exact locations of the pipes which carry the material to the Dodder are unknown. So nobody can be prosecuted and the local authorities can do no more than make a slow search for the sources and treat them one by one. Some day they will find them all and the Dodder will become clean once more.

The most serious case of pollution in the Dodder in recent times was the fish kill of 1987 when many thousands of trout died between the lower lake and Firhouse Weir. The lake had been drained for maintenance work and the drainage valve was left open. A heavy fall of rain caused a flood which swept enormous quantities of silt down through the outlet, silt which would normally stay on the bed of the lake without bothering anybody. But in the river it clogged the gills of the trout. What was more, the silt coated the stones and gravel of the stream bed, killing the food animals as well as the fish. This made it even more difficult for the fish population to recover. By 1990 all seemed well again and the minds of the Corporation workers involved were concentrated wonderfully.

Living space

The more uneven the stream bed, the more trout can live there. Their territorial disposition makes each individual try to chase all the others out of sight. Therefore, in a pool where the bed is level without any large stones or rocks sticking up, trout can see each other over a considerable distance and are kept very busy harassing their neighbours. This makes for two serious problems. Firstly all the trout have to keep very well spaced out and there is only room for small numbers of them. Secondly, they waste a lot of energy in this behaviour so that they need more food.

Where there are all sorts of irregularities in the stream, there are plenty of hiding places. The trout are out of sight of their neighbours and accordingly out of mind. Moreover, the rocks and stones give shelter from the main current and the trout are able to maintain their positions with a minimum of energy. So there is room for far greater numbers and the bigger population is also better fed: they can devote nearly all their energy to hunting.

The bigger the trout, the deeper the water they require. No matter how many big stones there may be on the bottom, they are of little use if the water is just a shallow trickle. The Dodder in a dry summer has a very low flow and steps have been taken to create pools for the fish. This has been done, among other places, below Spawell where a series of low weirs has been made by raking up the gravel. By the Lower Dodder Road and Orwell Park the pools are formed by concrete weirs.

Guardians of the fishes

The Fishery Act of 1848 established Boards Conservators for fisheries and the Dodder fell within the jurisdiction of the Dublin Fishery District. The Board was not greatly interested in the river, since it was responsible also for the salmon of the Liffey and the welfare of a small trout stream would have been a matter of little concern. The Dodder fishery began to be taken seriously in 1958 when a group of residents in the valley got together to found the Dodder Anglers' Club.

At that time fish kills caused by pollution were frequent and the trout population of the river was seriously depleted. Long before most people had even begun to think of Conservation, the Dodder Anglers mobilised to fight a relentless battle against the polluters. At the same time members of the Club devoted their weekends to physically cleaning up the river banks. The Fishery Act of 1959 incorporated a useful Section forbidding the discharge of material which could injure fish or the food of fish. This made the prosecution of offenders much easier than in former times.

The Anglers also had a meeting with the County Council at which they placed on the table before the assembled Councillors a bottle of 'sewage fungus': an unpleasing hairy grey mass composed of myriads of bacteria: enough bacteria, the Anglers claimed, to wipe out Tallaght. The Council took the hint and cooperated by embarking on a major effort to divert the offending waste to the sewerage system. One mystery fish killer remained for a long time. Finally it was traced to a bright clean shopping centre, kept that way with a particularly fierce detergent. This, together with the washings of the floor, was emptied daily into the unfortunate river until a vigilant Angler happened to come

Mallard

by one day when the cleaner was pouring his libation. The shopping centre management took prompt action and the Dodder finally came clean.

However, cleanliness was only part of the problem of keeping the Dodder filled with trout. The shortage of natural spawning facilities severely limits the numbers and that is why the Dodder Anglers supply the river with fish which have been spawned and reared in the Central Fisheries Board's trout farms at Roscrea and Mullingar. The fishing season opens on St Patrick's Day and, a little before that, trout of one or two pounds weight are released. A second stocking with big trout takes place later in the year and sometimes fry are supplied as well, to grow up on their own.

In 1990 the stocking operation began on 14th March, just before the opening of the season. Seven hundred two-year-old trout from the fishfarm were released over the whole length of the river from Bohernabreena downstream. Being over 9 inches long, these fish may all be kept by the anglers who catch them. Trout of less than that must be handled very carefully and returned at once to the water. In June 1,000 'summerlings', small trout a year and a half in age and less than 9 inches, were released. These live on natural food and grow big enough to catch the following year. From time to time fry, just a few months old, are also planted and sometimes also big trout between 2 pounds and 5 pounds.

Just about everybody who fishes in the Dodder is a member of the Anglers' Club. Membership numbers have been as high as 1,400 but 500 is nearer to the usual figure. They belong to a very interesting organisation. Basically the idea is to have a good fishery but the concept is immeasurably wider than that. A good fishery needs clean water and the pursuit of clean water awakens a deep respect for the entire environment. The fishing to some becomes a matter of minor importance, indeed there are very active members who don't actually fish — the maintenance of a bright river, easy to walk along, is an end in itself.

CHAPTER 8

Epilogue —
caring for the Dodder

This book makes only passing reference to one aspect of the Dodder. There are reaches where rusting supermarket trolleys are more in evidence than the unspoiled river bed, where the willows are festooned with multi-coloured plastic bags, where the paving under the bridges is scattered with broken glass and the lawns littered with soft-drink cans and the wrappings of convenience foods.

In too many places liquid, grey and stinking, pours from sewer pipes and discolours the water of the river. In others, eminently respectable gardeners throw their rubbish over the fence, out of their line of vision but painfully obvious to those who walk the far side of the valley. Burned-out cars and spoil from building sites mar many a potentially pleasant scene.

Who cares?

A great many people do — and that is why I concentrated on the good things of the valley and appeared to ignore the bad. The Dodder of the 19th century and even in the first half of the 20th was a great deal worse than in the 1990s. The improvement continues — and with increasing speed. The filth is transitory and in practical terms can be done away with very easily. The psychological problem is a little more difficult, but far from insoluble and the prognosis is excellent.

Local authorities

The positive approach to the Dodder began a century ago when the Rathmines Town Commissioners went to great lengths to beautify their property around the reservoirs, planting splendid trees and colourful shrubs and building delightful houses for their workers. In more recent times, a vital step was taken in the adoption of part of the Abercrombie Plan for Dublin in 1941:

> It is proposed to reserve parkway strips along the Dodder and the Tolka. In the case of the Dodder, it is a simple matter with the aid of a few light foot bridges to give direct access for pedestrians from Ballsbridge the whole way to the green belt.

How far this has been achieved in the fifty years since the plan was published can be seen by anyone who walks the Dodder downstream from Oldbawn. The goal of a footpath all the way along the riverside has not quite been attained, but the green strip of the 'linear park' is nearing completion. Meanwhile the process of aquiring the last remaining gardens and fields and making agreements with developers to preserve essential portions of land goes ahead steadily. Most of the time it is unobtrusive, dedicated work by officials of the two local authorities beavering away on legal complexities undreamed of by the majority of citizens.

Anglers

An important development in the work of voluntary organisations was the foundation of the Dodder Anglers' Club in 1958. Their members encouraged, to put it mildly, all the official bodies concerned to take seriously the problems of water pollution. One approach was to prosecute offending factories, the other to pipe effluents into the sewerage system rather than releasing them to the river.

Another major contribution of the Anglers was to curtail the vegetation along the banks. This is one of the perplexing problems in making the Dodder valley acceptable to all people — greens and not-so-greens alike. A high-minded ecologist would wish to leave the natural vegetation to establish itself all over. That would mean the development of an impenetrable scrub of hawthorn, blackthorn and other interesting native bushes. It would be good for some of the birds and for badgers and foxes but intolerable for other birds and inaccessible even for ecologists.

The fact is that beautiful river banks with lawn or pasture down to the margin and just the occasional alder or willow are artificial. This is a case where strict nature-preservation and the needs of human beings come into conflict and a balanced outlook must be developed. In the case of the Dodder, herons, grey wagtails, mallard and trout, as well as people, need a riverside uncluttered by bushes.

Volunteers

The latest development in care for the Dodder was the formation of a Dodder Valley Environment Group in 1990. The Group with the co-operation of FÁS set up a Social Employment Scheme to work on the river between Old Bawn and Firhouse, employing twenty-nine people for a year. Some of the twenty-nine are engaged in surveying the flora and fauna and geography of this part of the river, the others do the physical work of cleaning up. An essential feature of the project is to mount an information campaign to interest all residents, but young people in particular, in the values of the valley. Trees will be planted — but planted

High tide at London Bridge

by residents rather than by anonymous Council employees. The aim is to involve the whole community.

Voluntary groups such as this cannot replace the local authority work force — nor would they want to. Community involvement can do much to preserve the landscape, to save the trees from vandalism and to discourage the distribution of litter. The essential building and maintenance, however, require paid labour. What is more, parks sadly do not keep themselves. Litter breeds more litter: while in a well-kept park most people will actually use the bins and few will cut down trees. But park keepers need to be paid with public money. Hopefully, a well-informed public will be prepared to part with the same and that is the material side of the information campaign.

The future

Year by year more houses are built in the valley of the Dodder, new generations of children come to play by its banks. The roads of the housing estates are grey and dusty, the valley green and refreshing, a place of peace. In heroic times the Dodder thrilled to the hunt of the Fianna. Its floods killed the settlers of the 17th century. The industrialists of the 19th century nearly killed the river. Town planners, Parks Departments and the plain people are bringing it back to glorious life.

REFERENCES

P. Abercrombie. planning report commissioned by County Borough of Dublin and Neighbourhood, 1941.

E. Ball. *A History of the County Dublin.* (reprint) Gill and Macmillan, 1979.

M. Barry. *Across Deep Waters.* Frankfort Press, 1985.

G. Boate. *Ireland's Natural History.* (reprint 1860)

C. Boylan. *Herbert Park.* Dublin Corporation.

Giraldus Cambrensis. *Topography of Ireland.* J. J. O'Meara. translation, Dundalgan Press, 1951.

N. Colgan. *Flora of the County Dublin.* Hodges Figgis, 1904.

M. Craig. *Dublin 1660-1860.* The Cresset Press, 1952.

R. Goodwillie, M. Craig and R. Haworth. *Dodder Valley Survey.* A report for the Planning Department, Dublin County Council, An Foras Forbartha, 1973.

W. Handcock. *The history and antiquities of Tallaght.* (reprint) Tower Books, 1976.

P. Healy. *The valley of Glenasmole.* Dublin Historical Record 16, 1961, 109-129.

J. Hegarty. *The Dodder Valley.* Dublin Historical Record 1, 1939; 59-72.

P. Hennigan, J. McDaid and J. Keyes. *Dodder River – flood study.* Institution of Engineers of Ireland, 1988.

P. W. Joyce. *Irish names of places Vol ii.* Educational Co. of Ireland.

W. St. J. Joyce. *The neighbourhood of Dublin.* (reprint) Skellig Press, 1988.

J. M. Keyes. 'Hurricane Charlie — River Dodder flooding'. *The Engineer's Journal,* November 1987, 10-13.

G. W. Lamplugh and others. *The geology of the country around Dublin.* Memoirs Geological Survey of Ireland, 1903.

R. Mallett. *River Dodder District Report to the Commissioners on the Proposed Formation of Reservoirs on the River Dodder for the prevention of sudden floods, and accumulation of water for the constant supply of mills on that river and on the water-courses.* HMSO, 1844.

H. Morris. 'Where was Bruidhean Dá Derga?' *Journal of the Royal Society of Antiquaries of Ireland,* 5, 1935, 297-312.

E. O'Curry. *Ordnance Survey Letters.* Royal Irish Academy, 1837.

J. O'Daly. 'The chase of Loch Laen'. *Transactions of the Ossianic Society,* 4, 1859, 217-219.

J. O'Daly. 'Adventures of the Amadán Mór'. *Transactions of the Ossianic Society,* 6, 1861, 171-173.

L. O'Dea. 'The Fair of Donnybrook'. *Dublin Historical Record,* 19, 1952, 11-20.

W. Petty. *Hiberniae delineato, 1685.*

L. Price. *Place names of County Wicklow.*

J. Shannon. *Bushy Park Trail.* Dublin Corporation, 1979.

F. Synge. *The Glacial deposits of Glenasmole, County Dublin, and the neighbouring uplands.* Geological Survey of Ireland, Bulletin 1, 1971, 87-97.

C. Threlkeld. *Synopsis stirpium hibernicarum, Dublin, 1727.*

J. S. Turner. 'The Carboniferous limestone in Co. Dublin south of the River Liffey'. *Scientific Proceedings Royal Dublin Society*, 25, 1950, 169-192.

A. Tyrrell. 'Description of the Rathmines and Rathgar Township water works'. *Proceedings Institute of Mechanical Engineers*, 1888, 523-537.

MAPS

Besides the current editions of the Ordnance Survey, three 19th-century maps have provided invaluable information. All are available in reprints by Phoenix Maps.

1816 — John Taylor's map of the environs of Dublin.

1843 — Ordnance Survey 1:12,000 C. Dublin Sheet 22 (Rathfarnham)

1849 — Ordnance Survey 1:12,000 C. Dublin Sheet 18 (Dublin City)

UPDATE

Since this book was published in 1991, many changes for the better have taken place, one or two for the worse, and exciting plans for further improvements are closer to completion. The river is now under the jurisdiction of three local authorities: The Dublin Corporation property remains as it was, but South County now rules the left bank as far as the Castle Gate (p. 115) at which point Dún Laoghaire–Rathdown takes over.

At Castlekelly Bridge (p. 61) a much-needed car-park has been provided at the edge of the woodland on the right bank. The footpath on the same side of the upper lake has been greatly improved, and access to St Ann's churchyard made easier.

Oldbawn House (p. 79) has sadly perished in a sea of suburbia, but South County Parks Department are making great progress downstream of the bridge and have their sights set firmly on the land upstream. The sand martins (p. 83) have departed, probably disturbed simply by the numbers of people who had access to their nesting tunnels. There is a very exciting scheme to plant woodland, with beech and oak and such 'fruits of the forest' as apple and damson.

The old footbridge at Firhouse (p. 91), sadly, was replaced: though the red-painted replacement certainly has plenty of character. In the autumn of 1997 work began on making the waterside below the weir more accessible. Footpaths are being laid down by the water's edge and, ultimately, a passage will be made beneath the road to link up with the Cherryfield (p. 96) property downstream. More woodland will be planted here and the old hedges maintained. The highlight is the cowslip field, a brilliant sight in early summer, carefully nurtured by judicious mowing. Later in summer it becomes a meadow, resplendent with wild flowers.

One of the greatest achievements of the Corporation Parks people, has been the acquisition of five acres from their neighbouring nuns in Bushy Park (p. 108). The property boundary had cut one of the ponds in two and it has now been possible to remove the offending boundary wall. The water supply to the new pond has been changed: the original source was subject to pollution, but clean river water now flows there from the Dodder upstream. The Corporation was able to arrange for a riverside path on the left bank at Milltown (p. 123) under the new apartment blocks and is preserving from the housing developers the strip of three hectares which runs from Milltown to Clonskeagh Bridge (p. 126) on the left bank. This remains in private hands but is crying out for an injection of public money to place it in the hands of the citizens and the care of the Parks Department. Farther downstream, at Ballsbridge (p. 141), a new bridge has been built and access to Herbert Park maintained.

On the right bank, Dún Laoghaire–Rathdown authorities have been able to make great improvements around the weir at Packhorse Bridge (p. 125). Judicious use of planning powers has made room for a strip of land along the river and part of the old mill race has been exposed and a new footpath laid.

Thanks to Gerry Barry, Christy Boylan, Willy Connor, Ray Cullinane and Mary Keenan for bringing me up to date on the achievements and aspirations of the Parks Departments.

Christopher Moriarty
January 1998

The Book of the Liffey
From source to the sea

Edited by Elizabeth Healy, with texts by Christopher Moriarty
and Gerard O'Flaherty plus many supporting contributors

'Rarely can a river of eighty miles offer so much for discovery
from its peaty birth-pool to its industrial harbour.'

A detailed, illustrated account of all aspects of the Liffey and
its hinterland — its geological and geographical aspects, flora
and fauna, its folklore, history and literature. Lavishly illustrated with over 200 maps, photographs, prints and drawings.
A rare treat.

ISBN 0-86327-167-7 (hardback)

Byways rather than Highways
Exploring the Wilderness
Christopher Moriarty

A wonderful choice of new ways of getting to your ultimate
destination — if you have one. Thirty-eight routes traverse the
greater part of Ireland but assiduously avoid the main roads.
Includes maps and delightful pictures.

Many of the byways bring you to places far from the spots
normally thronged by tourists. Some routes follow rivers and
lakes while others wander round about the bog. All come
complete with favourite picnic spots or places to stay or get a
meal. This is the book for the person who has a week to spend
in Ireland and for the person with a lifetime to do the same.

ISBN 0-86327-373-4

Available from:
WOLFHOUND PRESS
68 Mountjoy Square
Dublin 1
Tel: +353 1 874 0354
Fax: +353 1 872 0207

Exploring Dublin

Wildlife, Parks, Waterways

Christopher Moriarty

Cities are built by people for people. The preservation of nature is not a priority of planners and even the open spaces are tamed by gardeners. In spite of all this, wild plants and animals thrive in all the cities of the world, and Dublin is no exception.

Christopher Moriarty invites us to wander with him along the banks of the Grand Canal, the Royal Canal, down by the Liffeyside, and through Trinity College, St Stephen's Green and many of the smaller parks. Along the way, he draws our attention to a host of birds, wild flowers, trees, insects and animals.

Exploring Dublin: Wildlife, Parks, Waterways is packed with background information too, on topics ranging from the construction of the canals and bridges, to the growth of St Stephen's Green, the history of Trinity College and the development of College Park.

Another beautifully illustrated book for all citizens
and lovers of nature.

ISBN 0-86327-590-7

Available from:
WOLFHOUND PRESS
68 Mountjoy Square
Dublin 1
Tel: +353 1 874 0354
Fax: +353 1 872 0207